Gentlemen in the Building Line

Gentlemen in the Building Line
The development of South Hackney

Isobel Watson

PADFIELD PUBLICATIONS

First published 1989
by Padfield Publications
Roland House
29 Stepney Green
London E1 3JX
(Telephone 01.791.2661)

British Library Cataloguing in Publication Data:
Watson, Isobel
   Gentlemen in the Building Line: the development of South Hackney
   1. London. Hackney (London Borough), History
   I. Title
   942.1'44

ISBN 0 9515003 0 9

The cover is a detail from a lithograph of Gascoyne Road, 1848, and is
reproduced by permission of the London Borough of Hackney,
Archives Department

Printed by Aldgate Press, London E1

"Curiously enough, people who live in the west or the south frequently speak of Hackney as a terra incognita, in spite of its antiquity and the fame in which it was once held..."
W. S. Clarke, The Suburban Homes of London (1881)

"Part of the above Premises are most eligibly situate for building, a Road being cut for that purpose...Gentlemen in the Building Line will find it well worth their attention."
South Hackney sale particulars (1791)

"The mid-Victorian builders of our city streets are, historically speaking, a lost tribe."
Sir John Summerson, The London Building World of the 1860's (1973)

Contents

Part Three: Gardens into Suburb

Part Four: Living in South Hackney

Endpiece

List of illustrations

The illustrations on pages 15-64, 84, and 110-114 are reproduced by permission
of the London Borough of Hackney, Archives Department.
The base detail on the maps on pages 74, 90 and 98 is reproduced by permission
of Alan Godfrey Maps.

Acknowledgements

First and foremost, this book could never have been begun without the consistent help and advice of the staff, past and present, of Hackney Archives Department. Particular thanks are due to Jean Wait, who also read and commented on the manuscript, and David Mander, whose encouragement and local knowledge have been invaluable. Sheila Kertesz, archivist to the Sir John Cass Foundation, and Michael Sparks, Clerk to the Governors of the Foundation, have afforded me co-operation and facilities well in excess of what I could have had any right or reason to expect, and I am extremely in their debt. Of the many London record offices and libraries whose staff have been unfailingly helpful I must also give special thanks to the searchroom staff at the Greater London Record Office and in particular those working on the St Thomas's Hospital estate records, the Guildhall Library archivists, Tower Hamlets Local History Library and the Huguenot Library.

My debt to Alan Godfrey, whose Godfrey Edition of old Ordnance Survey maps has in the past few years been of inestimable value to anyone interested in the evolution of urban areas, has been increased by his kind permission to use the base detail from his edition of the 1870 survey in preparing the new illustrative maps on pages 74, 90 and 98. Indeed the narrative is best understood with sheets 41 and 52 of the London series close at hand.

I am also very grateful to John Finn for his keen interest in the project and practical help with the cover. It is a subject for regret that it has proved impracticable to include more illustrative material, particularly photographs and estate plans. (Readers will find the defect alleviated by reference to David Mander's collection "The London Borough of Hackney in Old Photographs", published in autumn 1989 by Alan Sutton, and Elizabeth Robinson's excellent "Lost Hackney", published by the Hackney Society in September 1989.)

Many others have been generous with information which has assisted during the gestation period: I am particularly grateful to Dr Melvyn Brooks, Mr S.M. Shaanan, and to Colin and Sherry Bibby, who have all gone out of their way to give me access to otherwise unobtainable material; to Elizabeth Crawford, Lynne Blackmore and Andrew Byrne, from whose own special knowledge I have benefited; and to John Rayment and Jean Tooke for generously sharing with me their discoveries about their builder ancestors. Thanks also to the Revd. E. H. Jones for permission to copy certain parochial records.

There are bound to be errors in what has resulted; these are, needless to say, all my own work.

Stepney Green   *September 1989*

South Hackney estates

Key

1 - Hedger
2 - Mann
3 - Mills
4 - Leny Smith & Co.
5 - Poole's charity
6 - Ebenezer Johnston

7 - Samuel Matthews
8 - H. D. Hacon
9 - Hickling
10 - Crown
11 - William Bradshaw
12 - William Eagle
13 - Hambro' Synagogue
14 - Thomas Natt
15 - Parochial charities

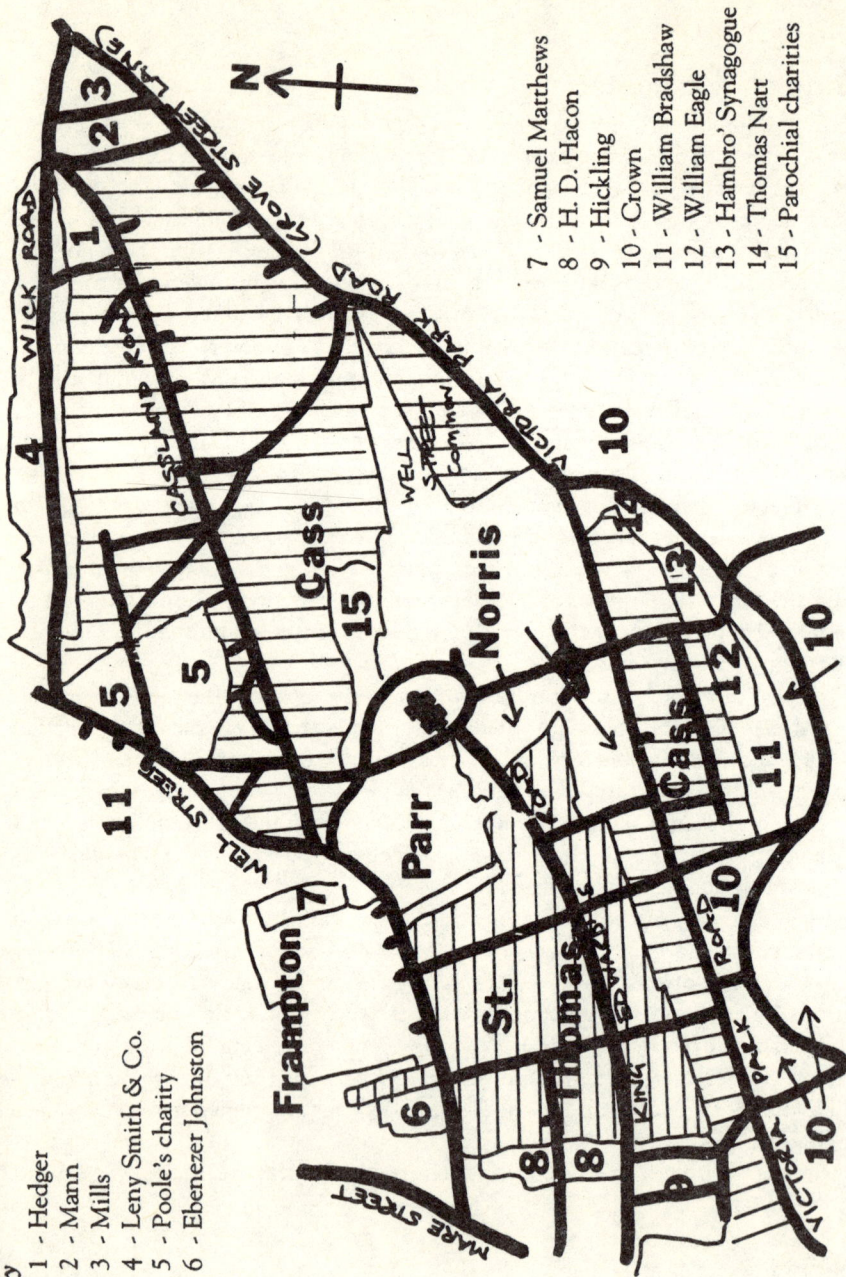

Introduction

The aim

As with any area as densely developed and populated, there are many books which could be written about South Hackney. This is only one of them, and it has the limited purpose of attempting to explain how South Hackney had come to take the shape it had, before the great changes of twentieth century redevelopment were brought to bear on it. I was driven to satisfy my own curiosity, as a local resident, about the built environment in my immediate neighbourhood, to which those who shaped it had left so many intriguing physical clues. Whose coats-of-arms were on the pediment of the Georgian terrace in Cassland road? Were they those of the trustees of · Sir John Cass's charity, generally believed to have built the terrace? (They were not; and they didn't.*) Was there a connection between "Percy villas" in Well street, and the houses two streets away, in Tudor road, which had such remarkable similarities amidst an intervening wilderness of differences? (As it happened, there was.**) Why at one end of this tiny parish did we have a couple of thoroughly urban, early Victorian streets that would not be out of place in Chelsea (Warneford and Fremont streets) and at the other a contemporary slice of villagey variety (Brookfield road) more reminiscent of Hampstead? Who, indeed, were the originators of this diversity, and why was it so diverse?

I soon concluded that the built pattern could only be understood by reference to the individual or corporate purpose behind the development of the various estates into which the area was divided at the time of systematic development, and that the area's diversity arises essentially from the fragmented nature of local landownership. If the landowners' purposes can be read at times only elusively, at least "the big three", as they might be called - Sir John Cass's charity, St Thomas's hospital, and the Norris family - have left, or retain, what is for the most part remarkably full documentary material, although the devolution of the smaller, more fragmented parcels of land in the earliest settled parts is sometimes, on presently available information, impossible to trace.

Part One, which deals with building development in the 18th century, contains material which may be of interest beyond Hackney. It demonstrates that - whatever the assumption about the length of leases in central London - the usual length of a building lease in the area, as elsewhere in Hackney, was 51 years at the close of the 18th century and by the end of the 19th still only 80 or, sometimes, 90 years[1]. It also discusses the lack of system, purpose and indeed expertise of estate owners seeking building development at this time, and the haphazard quality of development when and where it took place. The principal physical survival of this era is Hackney terrace (20-54 Cassland road), Hackney's finest remaining Georgian building, the financial arrangements for which were along building society lines, an unusual feature in a London palace terrace with evident social aspirations.

* see page 32.   **see page 73.

Part Two deals with the context and framework of systematic estate development in the 19th century, following the informal redefinition of the area by the building of the Regent's canal around 1820 and the laying out of Victoria park in the early 1840's. This Part attempts to give an outline of the relative importance to the shape of the area both of individual developments and co-operation between estate owners. It describes the framework within which 19th century building arrangements took place, with examples which look forward to later chapters. It takes a step back from the narrative, and because of its examples could as usefully be read, if only for the examples, by anyone already familiar with the functioning of land development in towns, after Part Three as before it.

But principally this book consists of the answers to my original quest, the story, largely, of the Victorian survivals, which is contained in Part Three, and the influence that the size and policies of the various estate owners have had on what is now to be seen. The clearest, if most obvious, lesson is the influence of fragmented early ownership at focal points such as the oldest settlements, at Tudor road and Mare street, Well street and Grove street; echoed in the fragmentation and lack of continuity of the smaller estates developed in the 19th century. On the one hand, lax estate management has also played its part; on the other, the beneficial effect of increasing professionalisation of management, particularly by the Cass estate, cannot be underestimated.

This story is brought to an end, more or less arbitrarily, in 1900. Indeed by 1880 the search for ever more building land was nearly over and the transformation of market gardening area into comfortable suburb nearly complete. All that remained was minor infilling, made possible by the demise of one or two less than remarkable 18th century houses; and the sacrifice of a few, perhaps all too large, back gardens.

The other factor which affects the present face of South Hackney, the major redevelopment following bomb devastation or, to a lesser extent, slum clearance (the Kingshold estate, Frampton Park and the ancient centre of Well street) is, of course, a different story, although one which has obscured, by obliterating carefully devised 19th century street patterns, part of the evidence on the ground of the intentions of the area's original developers. The result is particularly sorry in the case of the GLC's Kingshold estate, which has removed the fine view of the west front of the church of St John of Jerusalem which required the co-operation of two major estates to bring about.

Part Three demonstrates not only that the shape of South Hackney was to a great extent the result of such co-operation, itself obscuring earlier field patterns; but that the estates had a learning curve to climb in seeking to control the building operations they fostered.

Because Parts One to Three are about buildings, Part Four deals, for the sake of perspective, with the people who lived in the buildings, and some of the factors which will have affected life in South Hackney during the 19th century. It does not pretend to be comprehensive; in the absence of a detailed quantitative study it can only be impressionistic.

The area

This is a study of South Hackney: but not of all of South Hackney. I have defined the area more narrowly than the historic parish, formally established in 1825 from the southerly, and by then long informally recognised as natural, division of the ancient parish of St John at Hackney, and concentrated around the old settlements at both ends of Well street and in Grove street (the latter now Lauriston road). Even by the time of the partition the positioning of the boundary may have seemed a little strange, separating as it did St Thomas's square from St Thomas's chapel and St Thomas's place, and otherwise creating what must have, with the disappearance of field boundaries into Loddiges nursery, have seemed to be an artificial division of the St Thomas's hospital lands. Nonetheless, a study such as this needs to be contained within some limits, and to the north at least the parish bounds have proved the most convenient, not least because post-war development has itself created a stylistic break in the streetscape. To the south, the creation of Victoria Park contrived a green belt for South Hackney.

I have also left out everything west of Mare street; other than in passing, I have not dealt with development of so much of the parish as lies on the east side of London Fields, largely because the dramatic influence of the railway on the physical character of this pocket of the parish is such as to make it worthy of a study of its own.

Equally I have not dealt extensively with Hackney Wick. From the days - over by 1840 - of the silk mills, the 19th century story of the Wick was a specialised one, one of the vagaries of manufacturing industry - often of a noxious character - and its chicken-and-egg relationship with the impoverishment of the local population. Work has recently been done on the industrial archaeology of the area, and work remains to be done on its social history. Today the separation effected by railway and motorway underscores more than ever the distinctness of most of this part from the remainder of the parish. Anyone looking for a discussion of the development of the area east of Cadogan terrace, or north of Wick road, will therefore find very little in what follows.

The third exclusion is everything south of the canal: in other words, Northiam Street and the surroundings of the Triangle. Again, physically this is cut off from the remainder, and there is little that is left even of its 19th century character. I refer to it in passing, but, in the light of the general aim, only in so far as it sheds any light on what was happening to the north and east.

What then is included? We are dealing with the area east of Mare street and straddling Well street, to the northerly parish limit created by reference the boundaries of long-lost fields; towards the east Well street itself, beyond its northerly bend, becomes the boundary or runs very close to it. From there we follow the old line of the now subterranean Hackney brook, eastwards to the furthest tip of Victoria

Park. From there the southern boundary snakes westwards through the Park, still based on other, long-disappeared field boundaries (which to this day dictate the boundary between Hackney and Tower Hamlets), westwards to the canal and to Mare street again.

I have concentrated on buildings, and even streets, which still exist at the expense of those which have been lost; for this reason this study deals only sketchily with the 19th century development of the Frampton Park estate and Wick road, to name but two.

Using the book

Central to following the discussion in the text are the maps, beginning with an extract from John Rocque's map (opposite), made from his survey of the mid-1740's, and Starling's map (page 50), of 1831. The latter , although only reproduced here in detail, shows the sporadic building of the late 18th century, and clearly indicates how broadly accurate, within its limits, Rocque's map was. The terrain in fact changed very little between his time and the 1840's, when the large estates began systematic development. Turner's map, page 64, gives the area as it was immediately before development began.

Most essential however is the estate map (page 10), which shows the principal estates into which South Hackney was divided as they stood in the mid-19th century. It represents no precise date; as will be shown in Part Three there was so much interchange of marginal strips between estate owners (not always readily capable of precise delineation to scale) that to select any particular date would be more misleading than to give a conspectus of the estates as each of them stood immediately after development, as this map attempts to do.

No apology is made for inconsistency in the approach to street names. For the sake of comprehension, it is sometimes most convenient to use the modern name of a street - for example, Warneford street, and separate parts of it, have in their time had several names use of which would add nothing to clarity of exposition. Where however the length or shape of a street has changed, this is indicated by use principally of the original name, such as St Thomas's road for the whole length of the road that exists now in two truncated stretches as Ainsworth road and Skipworth road.

Use of the original name of a street is on occasion the only way of ensuring accuracy: the old line of Grove street, for example, is not identical with the modern line of Lauriston road. In other instances an old name aids identification: Victoria Park road in its modern extent has two distinct halves, either side of the Lauriston road roundabout. The modern, western section has never had any other name, which is used here; but Grove street lane is used for the older, eastern section, which had various names of which this was the most persistent in the relevant period. If this is found initially confusing, the glossary in Appendix 1 has been designed to help.

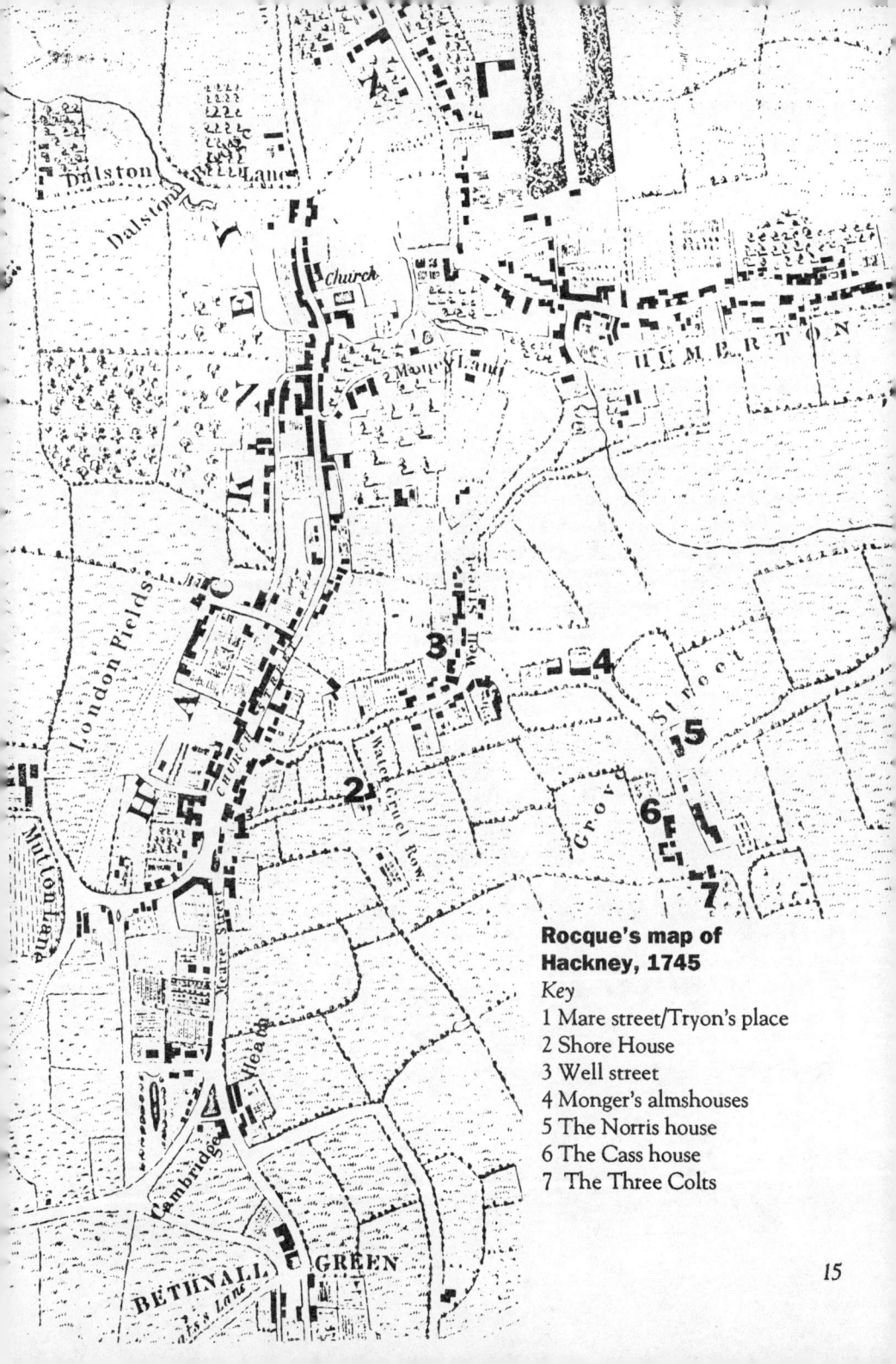

Rocque's map of Hackney, 1745

Key

1 Mare street/Tryon's place
2 Shore House
3 Well street
4 Monger's almshouses
5 The Norris house
6 The Cass house
7 The Three Colts

Part One: Estate Development in the 18th Century

Before Development

We have, from John Rocque's map, a reasonably good idea of the shape of Hackney about 1745, and for some hundred years afterwards. Like Bethnal Green directly to the south, it was a village settlement, in ribbon form. There were two main concentrations: around the church, and on the east side of London Fields, from which Well street lay eastwards. It was at once sufficiently remote from the City to be a village, and accessible enough to be reached on foot. Thus it had become famous as the home of boarding schools for pupils of both sexes, and as a pleasure resort for casual and summer visitors from the City.

South Hackney was separated from the central village by the length of a field or two. Leaving aside the cluster west of Mare street, with which this study will not be dealing, the two main areas of settlement were in Well street. Grove street (the area to the south of the crossroads between Victoria park road and Lauriston road) was tiny; not even comparable with the crossroads settlements of Dalston and Kingsland further west. It was originally a cluster of cottages round a small group of houses belonging to City merchants, and not even connected by road with Bow until relatively late.

One concentration of buildings clustered around the junction with Mare street (originally Meare street, on account - according to one theory - of its bogginess; the main thoroughfare both to Hackney village and to London), and that of Mare street with Tryon's place near the Triangle. A residence here would be described as a residence in or at Mare street. The other, known as Well street, was a settlement probably of medieval origin round the reputed site of the old well which gave the street its name, on the north side of Well street near its junction with Grove street. Here stood an ancient building, said to have been the house of the priors of the Knights of St John of Jerusalem, established in Clerkenwell, who had succeeded to the property of the Knights Templar. This house, increasingly fragmented until during the 19th century it disappeared into or under other construction, was a small brick double-fronted building with crow-stepped gables, observed in the 1790's to be "inhabited by chimney sweepers" - perhaps suggesting to an earlier and neighbouring publican the name given to his hostelry, the "Two Black Boys"[2]. The settlement here was early associated with the Common; hence the name by which the common fields came to be known.

Principally Rocque's map shows fields; what it does not show is what was produced in those fields. South Hackney was, at that time and throughout the remainder of its time prior to development, primarily a market gardening area, its economy heavily dependent on supplying the capital with field and orchard produce. Gardens framed each side of Mare street, south of the Triangle; they stretched south of the lane (at this time known as Grove street lane) which ran from Grove street to the Wick and which now forms the eastern arm of Victoria park road. The garden ground south of this lane, together with one of the area's three nurseries, was eventually swallowed up by the Park, its fruit trees cut down lest they provide an inducement to thieving and disorder[3]. Around the present site of Queen Anne and Kenton roads, John Shoobert or Shuport held 3 acres on which he ran a seedsman's business which advertised London-wide. Presumably he or his family were settlers from continental Europe, like John Busch and Conrad Loddiges, who successively ran a nationally famous nursery on the St Thomas's estate north of Well street[4].

Well street Common, often just called the "common field", was in use mainly for arable crops; like the other Hackney commons, from the Marshes to the Downs, it was "Lammas land", giving the commoners the right to turn their beasts out to graze in between the cutting of the crops around "loaf mass", or lst August, and 25th March (old calendar), after which re-sowing would take place. Originally, no doubt, common rights extended only to inhabitants of the manor (in this case the Hackney manor of Lordshold), but by the end of the 18th century grazing rights were asserted for all inhabitants of the parish[5].

As was characteristically the case with Lammas land, Well street common was in multiple ownership, its four separate fields by the end of the 17th century having come into the hands of three separate copyhold owners, the Cass family (the northern and southern field), the Norris family (the middle field) and the trustees for the Hackney parochial charities (the western field), this last field having been bought in 1694 to endow charities for the Hackney poor out of bequests by Richard South and Esther White. Until well after intensive development of the area began, the parish field was used as meadowland, and the remainder for arable crops, being let on yearly tenancies to local farmers and cowkeepers[6].

North of the track from Well street to the Wick which became Cassland road lay grazing meadows running down to the Hackney brook. A terrace of three houses of late 18th century origin called Heart place, which stood just to the west of the present junction with Kenton road, later formed the premises of the local cowkeeper; and the butcher at Homerton grazed his cattle here[7]. South of the road`were substantial gravel pits and tracts of brick earth.

Meadowland extended westwards from Grove street; on the site of Connor street were later the premises of another cowkeeper, William Eagle. A substantial brickfield lay south of the present Wetherell road (later a row of cottages called Providence row); it also mostly disappeared into the park.

Like much of east London, there is a high water table, and a good deal of surface water. There were ponds by the brook at Morning lane (commonly known as "Water lane" at this point, although Rocque has "Money lane") and another at the southern end of Grove street - hence Lauriston road swings round at its southern point, where the only watery relic is now a Metropolitan Cattle-trough Association horse-trough (initialled to commemorate twenty five years of all but anonymous Victorian marriage).

The oldest man-made features of any area are likely to be its highways; Mare street and Morning lane are such, and Well street, following in all probability the line of a tributary of the Hackney brook, is another. All these date from long before written record. Grove road, on the other hand, was originally a path through fields leading to Grove street, and is as to the southern part of its extent referred to as a new road in 1804[8].

A subsidiary road was almost exactly co-extensive with the modern Shore road, and originated not as a public highway but as the approach to Shore house, otherwise Shoreditch place house, the principal house (though not the physical centre) of the so-called manor of the same name, a collection of landholdings east of Mare street and at Clapton acquired from the 14th century onwards by the Shordych family, and conveyed to the Governors of St Thomas's hospital on its 16th century re-foundation.

On or near the site of a house originally known as Grove house, and thus possibly related in origin to Grove street, by the early 18th century the house had become known as Shore place or Shore house. It could be reached not only by the spur road leading southwards a short distance from Well street, described at that time as a "passage", but by a track, on the line of Tudor road, approached through a narrow gap at the west end, leading from Mare street and known as Tryon's place, from "the "several handsome houses" built there in the mid-17th century by Thomas Tryon. Beside Shore house, old and decaying by Rocque's time, were cottages called Water gruel row, which survived the old house itself[9].

Other settlement was in clusters of houses around the Triangle, in ribbon fashion along Mare street, and around a few large houses in Grove street; for the most part these latter faced each other east and west, to the south of the site of the present roundabout. These were the country houses of City merchants, including that of Sir John Cass, founder of the educational charity in Aldgate, and his father. This house, on or near the site of one formerly "known by the sign of the George", was later occupied by Peter Thellusson, whose successful attempt to create by will an accumulation of income across several generations of his family led to Parliamentary intervention in the form of the Accumulations Act 1800, the so-called "Thellusson Act"[10].

North-east of the Cass house, approximately where Penshurst road opens to the east, stood the mansion belonging to several generations of Henry Norrises. The first of the family to settle in Hackney, Hugh Norris, in 1653 bought a rambling, turreted house then about a century old; his grandson, the first Henry, rebuilt it in classical fashion in 1729. It was the family's country home until Henry Norris III (b. 1734) removed to Woodford. His son, however, the Revd. Henry Handley Norris, South Hackney's first rector, ministered to his parish from here. The Norrises' thirty acres lay west and east of Grove street and included the middle field of the Common.[11]

At the foot of the hamlet, and facing the southerly traveller was the Three Colts tavern and tea-garden, accessible by path from Bethnal Green across Bishop Bonner's fields, the ancient deer park that by the early nineteenth century afforded the most accessible open space for the mushrooming population of East London.

Well north of the hamlet, and regarded as part of Well street, were the almshouses established in 1669 under a bequest of Henry Monger, himself owner of much of the neighbouring land which came into the hands of the Cass family after his death. Before the building of Hackney terrace, it seems that another track to the Wick took the northerly side of the Common eastwards from these almshouses. At the Wick itself were Leny Smith's silk mills, and Wick House, at this time probably the most magnificent of the large mansions of the area. The silk mills were to endure no longer than 1840 but they, together with Berger's paint factory established near Morning lane in 1780, had more significance as a pointer to Hackney's future character than either Wick house or the Norris mansion.

St John of Jerusalem's Palace. HACKNEY.
Now Inhabited by· CHIMNEY SWEEPERS.

19

Landownership

The pattern of landownership in South Hackney, so far as traceable, changed little between the time of Rocque's survey and the beginning of systematic development. Even then, where freeholds are concerned, there was little change until the 1920's. Firm evidence of ownership patterns is only available for the very largest estates. Intervening development was on a small scale, and largely restricted to the three ancient centres of settlement: the nucleus of Grove street; Well street around the Prior's house; and the settlement around Tryon's place and the western end of Well street where it joins Mare street.

The most accurate picture we have is that provided by the tithe survey of 1843[12]. This was undertaken by special Commissioners, appointed under the Act of 1836 which provided for the commutation of tithes - a tax on crop-bearing land for the benefit of the church, hitherto payable in kind - into sums of money. As`always where taxation is concerned, great pains were taken to measure and describe accurately who owned what. As it happened, in South Hackney this exercise took place immediately before a substantial part of the area was engulfed by Victoria Park, and only four years before large tracts of land let on long leases in the 1780's reverted to owners eager to develop them. Thus it provides a reliable profile of the area immediately before its character changed for ever.

South Hackney parish proper consisted of a little over 402 acres; leaving out the area west of Mare street, and that east of where roads and rail now cut through Hackney Wick, this is reduced to a little over 320. Within this figure, the survey did not concern itself with holdings without significant cultivated land attached to any dwelling (the smallest holding assessed in the area east of Mare street is one of the middle houses in Hackney terrace, together with its garden, at 8 perches or 242 square yards). There is, therefore, no possibility of knowing the true number of landowners. The area of land thereby necessarily excluded amounts however to no more than 10 acres, and consists entirely of small huddles of houses at the three ancient centres of settlement.

This unknown number aside, the remaining total - 58 different owners - conceals the most striking profile of the area, which is that over 60 per cent of it belonged to only four different owners. Sir John Cass's charity estate, the largest of all, put together in the mid-17th century by Sir John's father, consisted of 76.23 acres, leaving aside the charity's holdings over the parish boundary in St Matthew, Bethnal Green as well as its substantial lands in Hackney marshes. Those of the Norris family, bought in 1652, and St Thomas's hospital consisted of 33.68 and 31.19 acres respectively. Thus nearly half of the area had continuity of ownership as far back as the mid 17th century - in the case of St Thomas's, for over a century longer.

The fourth largest holding was some 51.46 acres, the property of the heirs of

William Thompson of Stamford Hill. Like the Cass holdings in Bethnal Green parish, every last morsel of this property disappeared into the eastern end of Victoria Park - the owners sold up quickly to the Crown, who were then left to buy out the leases of the six market gardening businesses active on what became the eastern section of the Park[13].

We can add to this list a further dozen estates of more than three acres, of which the five abutting or straddling the Bethnal Green boundary - those of Captain Sotheby, John Ball and Charles Wells, amounting in total to 25.26 acres, and the 20.08 acres belonging to John Ridge and Samuel Mills - were also largely or wholly engulfed by the Park. Indeed by the time its land purchases were complete the Crown estate had acquired nearly a third of the acreage of the area for the Park, including 13 acres of brickfield.

Some 10.29 acres, either side of Wick road and around the Wick itself, were at the time of the tithe survey held by an insurance company, successors of the silk manufacturers Leny Smith and Co., who had gone out of business around 1840. At one time the mills at the Wick were reputedly the largest silk mills in the country, employing some seven hundred workers, mostly female; the buildings themselves were, after the demise of the silk trade, turned over to a small-scale rag, flock and horsehair business, and the associated dye works, once famous for their scarlet cloth, had closed altogether. Like the Spitalfields weaving trade, the business had fallen victim to increased mechanisation in the industry and to foreign competition let loose by the lowering of import duties[14].

The Norris family house in Grove street, about 1845

About half the size of the former Leny Smith estate were the combined holdings near Grove street of the trustees of two Jewish burial grounds. One, bought by the congregation of the Hambro' synagogue, the first schismatic offshoot of the Great Synagogue at Aldgate, to supplement their existing space at Hoxton, was laid out as a cemetery from 1788 onwards; it still forms part of the streetscape of Lauriston road. The other belonged to the Spanish and Portuguese Synagogue, and was designed to be let until their Mile End road ground had been filled up. This was lost to the encroaching Park.

Other land was held for different purposes of a public nature. Most of the Common belonged either to the Cass or the Norris estate, and was let for arable farming, but the western arm, behind Groombridge road, was held by the parish authorities in trust for the South Hackney poor, and let for grazing. (As the tenant of "Common House", which stood on the present site of Meynell gardens, was usually prepared to take it himself at more than the market rent to secure a pleasant southerly aspect, and to lay out an enlarged turning circle for his carriage in front of the house, the poor benefited by more than the market rent, at the price of minor enclosure of the Common[15].)

The right of administration of Monger's charity, previously exercised by the Cass trustees, was asserted successfully in 1800 by the parish authorities. They were also trustees of the bequest of Valentine Poole, who had in 1664 left "the Buttfield", east of Well street, for the benefit of the poor of the parish - the two roads bearing his name now bisect this field[16]. Altogether, the parish managed some 9.38 acres, leaving aside church and rectory land itself.

The daughters of the recently deceased Algernon Frampton, a physician, lived in a large old house on the north side of Well street, more or less opposite where Balcorne street was later opened up; they had inherited almost 10 acres. John Parr, a City cooper, held some 5.7 acres facing their property across the street; Zillah Hickling had some 3.67 acres lying just east of Mare street. The Reverend Thomas Mann and Samuel Mills each owned adjacent three acre plots at Hackney Wick. The earlier ownership of these several estates (other than Parr's, which at least around the latter part of the 18th century belonged to a family called Wowen) is not readily traceable.

It is with the development of these various estates for building, as well as those of the larger landowners, that what follows is mainly concerned; but it will be found that significant development proposals on the smaller as well as the larger estates did not materialise before the 1840's.

The 18th century estates

The lease

In the 18th century land use in Hackney was agricultural or horticultural, and interest in building development only sporadic. The Norrises, even as owner-occupiers, let what fields they did not require as parkland to local farmers; the Cass trustees, and the governors of St Thomas's hospital, each from their greater distance did the same.

St Thomas's managed the estate through its surveyor, who reported to its Grand Committee, which dealt with estate management matters for its extensive portfolio, countrywide. So far as the Cass property was concerned, there might be an annual inspection of the boundaries by a carefully prepared delegation sallying forth from Aldgate (a trip to inspect charity property at Hackney Marsh could be expected to entail a good dinner at, say, the Adam and Eve in Homerton[17]); but in either case management was little more than a matter of finding a tenant in whose interest it might be to manage the property on a day-to-day basis, and then ensuring that the rent was paid.

Both estates tended therefore to be let in segments as large as there were tenants to take them. Only the pressure of development potential led to splitting up. The Shoreditch place manor, South Hackney and Clapton holdings together, were let as a whole until the 1660's, the southern portion thereafter being identified as two parts, the smaller of which was split off to facilitate the development eastward of Tryon's place.

If a building lease was sought (and the only estates for which evidence of these survives are those of Cass and St Thomas's Hospital), then the investor required a term of years sufficient to secure a return on his outlay; but this was very much shorter than would be expected today. Of course, both the length of the lease and the rent it would command were the product of market forces, being set by prospective tenants' tenders, which in the case of the Cass estate the trustees took orally at a meeting at their offices in Aldgate[18]. And before building was an economic proposition, a copyhold landowner, such as the Cass or Norris estate, would have to free the land of its manorial constraints. Otherwise the length of the possible lease was limited by custom, and a "fine" payable to the Lord of the Manor on transfer. In Hackney this meant a lease of no more than 31 years, too short to secure sound building from an investor[19]. Despite the apparent control vested in the Lord of the manor transfer was more or less perfunctory, but it was essential to sound and substantial development that the developer's interest was sufficiently long - in the late 18th century, although commercial leases might vary very little from modern expectations, 51 years for house-building would be an acceptable minimum in Hackney[20]. From that time on, developers' expectations grew.

Between 1779 and 1786, the Cass trustees let the whole of their Hackney estate. To free the land of copyhold restraint they had enfranchised in 1783; even thereafter the sale of freeholds would have been insecure, being challengeable by charity beneficiaries (from time to time perceived as any parishioner of Aldgate). The leases in fact granted were for terms ranging from 21 to 61 years, according to whether the lessee was himself making a significant investment, and therefore seeking a longer term[21]. This was not a "building lease" in the more developed sense of being conditional on his attaining any particular stage or standard of building; the only return expected was a royalty on minerals extracted, in the knowledge that the estate's eastern extent in particular was rich in sand and gravel. The St Thomas's leases of this period were, by contrast, expressed to be in consideration of building, but even they were not apt for enforcement of such a covenant[22].

From the mid-18th century the standard term for a building lease from St Thomas's hospital was 51 years, unless some special circumstance (such as the need to synchronise neighbouring leases with a view to facilitating redevelopment later) indicated a different, shorter period. Commercial lettings - whether for chapels or market gardens - tended to be for 21 or 31 year terms, as did any leases of existing houses which were in sufficiently good condition for a tenant to be expected to undertake repairs, after the end of the builder or speculator's term.

Whereas the St Thomas's building agreement of 1768 for the Shore place redevelopment, like the contemporary lease to Robert Collins for the building of St Thomas's square, contemplated a 51 year term (with option to renew), by 1805 Hospital lettings had lengthened to 61 years. In that year "ground in Well street" was let to Thomas Pearson (for the first terrace in St Thomas's place) for that term, and in 1810 the site of the Paragon went to Robert Collins on a similar basis.

By the 1840's, when the Cass leases fell in and both the Cass trustees and the Governors of St Thomas's hospital were contemplating comprehensive development, a further encroachment in the developer's favour is apparent. The standard length of their lease had crept up to 75 years; the upward trend in the intervening period is evident on the Dalston and Upper Clapton estate of the Lord of the Manor, the Tyssen family. In South Hackney, after 1853, 80 years became the norm. This term was also the preference for the Cass estate from the 1840's until their final phase of 19th century development[23].

Thus in Hackney a builder might in the later 1700's expect a lease no longer than had been common on the Bedford estate in Bloomsbury or the expectation of the Grosvenor estate's contractors earlier in the century, although henceforth the 99-year term was becoming the norm on the great central estates, as indeed it is found occasionally in Hackney where the ground landlord is particularly anxious to secure development on a relatively limited acreage. Otherwise the terms granted in Hackney are in fact broadly commensurate, taking the hundred or so years beginning in the mid-1780's, with those for comparable properties built south of the river, in

Shore House, 1738

Camberwell, during the same period[24].

There is no evidence that these shorter terms were in themselves insufficient to secure a respectable standard of building, any more than that a uniform standard could be expected from every builder who took a mid-19th century 80 year building lease.

The St Thomas's estate and the development of Shore place

The land lying south of Well street, between the modern Shore place (not to be confused with the earlier road of that name, which is identical with the modern Shore road) and Kingshold road formed part, as far south as approximately the extent of the present Kingshold estate, of a series of scattered landholdings in Hackney acquired during the 14th century by the family of Elena and Sir John de Shordych[25].

Passing through marriage into the Tey family, then successively of the Crown and the Savoy Hospital, the Shordych lands came to form part of the endowment of the re-founded St Thomas's hospital, being given by Edward VI to the City Corporation as its Governors in association with the re-foundation of the hospital in 1551[26]. At this time, the so-called "manor of Shoreditch place" (as it came to be called during the 17th century, long after the Shordych family had relinquished it[27]) consisted not only of the land south of Well street on which undoubtedly some medieval building had subsisted, but other tracts east of Mare street (including the site of the present Devonshire and Darnley roads) and at Lower Clapton. Though described as a manor, there does not appear to be any subsisting evidence of there having been a manorial court.

By the early 18th century the "manor house called Shoreditch place" (of which a bleak pen and ink drawing survives, of a house with five angular bays) was alternatively known as Shore place (a term which equally extended to the immediate neighbourhood) or Shore house[28]. In 1715 it was occupied, perhaps among others,

25

by the relatively well-to-do relatives of the diarist Dudley Ryder[29], but thereafter by several very poor families. In 1720 it was noted as "old and out of repair" - the yearly tenant expecting the hospital to put in two new pumps and repair the old one[30] - and it finally disappeared in 1767-8, although the name (various as ever) evidently attached to the general neighbourhood of the old house for some time after it had gone[31].

A number of small tenements known as Water gruel row, so-called both on Rocque's map and in a lease of 1789, stood to the east of the present Shore road, at that time merely the "passage" to the old house, and housed the labourers who worked the orchards, paddocks and "pightle" of the house for market gardeners[32].

Development of the site started with Thomas Flight, "citizen and carpenter", previously a developer of hospital property in the City and a considerable land speculator in London and the country. In 1768 the Governors of St Thomas's Hospital granted him a 51 year repairing lease at the hefty rent of £110 for the 33 acres and shrewdly included an option to renew for 21 years, in consideration of his proposing to build "5 or 6 new tenements" at a cost to himself of £6,000. This agreement did in fact, over time, produce a few more than the 5 or 6 stipulated for, in the form of three large houses (including the one later known as "the Eagles") fronting Well street, and a terrace of 4 or 5 houses along the east side of the present Shore road[33]. A larger house to the south and east, near the later line of King Edward's road, ultimately known as Shore House, was built for and let to Flight's subtenant, the City hat wholesaler Gedaliah Gatfield, who was in occupation of premises in Shore place from 1767[34]. Of all these buildings no. 18 Shore road is the only survivor at the time of writing - if survivor it can be called.

A smaller scale development took place in 1789, just after the 21 year point when Flight exercised his option to extend the lease, and so arranged the matter that the holding was split between himself and Gatfield. A group of small houses, one becoming a shop, were built to the south of the earlier terrace, near the presumed site of Shoreditch place house.

Hackney Wick in 1831

This small development Flight sublet to Thomas Hamilton, trimmings manufacturer of St James's[35]. Thereafter, apart from the possible addition of a further house to the first Shore road terrace, and the building, to the south, of a nonconformist chapel on a 31 year lease in 1810-11, systematic landowners' development in this neighbourhood ended until the 1840's. Small-scale development on the more northerly part of the St Thomas's Hackney estate continued actively throughout the late century, in particular with Spackman's buildings (244-252 Mare street), of 1780-1, and in the early years of the next, with St Thomas's place (1805-7) and the Paragon (1810).

The Cass leases of the 1780's

Most of the individuals who took Cass or St Thomas's leases in the 18th century were not seeking windfall gains of the kind that came to be associated with speculative building in Victorian times. For the most part they were smallholders looking for pasture or garden ground; or a City businessman interested in securing control of the back land to his large Grove street villa, or looking for a steady investment income from subletting for farming. This, in effect, enabled the ground landlord to leave day to day management to the tenant who was prepared to take the trouble of finding sub-tenants to take grazing or arable land in small, affordable parcels.

The estates maintained, in other words, no employees to take an active role in estate management. There might be a retained surveyor; St Thomas's hospital had such extensive landholdings that a small part only of the surveyor's time could be allowed f or Hackney. Conversely, with the Cass estate, over and above a modest retainer for such matters as advising on minor repair work, such as to the Cass schoolroom at Aldgate, he would be paid professional fees as and when he was consulted. The Cass charity's own surveyor towards the end of the century, Jesse Gibson (who lived on the west side of Grove street in a house built, in pursuance of an agreement for a lease dated 1788, roughly where the Trinity Chapel now stands) would have been interested not only in any return from his lease of the fields which stretched westwards from his house, but in managing them as his private grounds. Gibson's own approach to matters was very leisurely, allowing 20 of his own 61 year term to elapse before requesting that the lease be granted in accordance with his agreement with the estate[36].

Where possible the Cass trustees let the whole of the estate for a sufficient period to encourage good management from the tenant; in the 1760's and 1770's this meant 21 year terms or the customary maximum of 31. Other than Jesse Gibson, who appears to have built a house which he and his family occupied successively at least until the late 1840's, the lessees were James Kerons and Charles Greenwollers, who were probably responsible for the building of five or six modest terraced houses on either side of Grove street on 61 year leases; and James Pickbourne, the tenant of the old Cass house on the west side, and (like Gibson) of some back land, who established a long-running boys' school on this site[37].

A substantial part of the Cass holding, totalling almost 70 acres of land in Hackney marsh as well as South Hackney, had been let as a whole in 1765 to a local farmer, Joseph Sureties, and indeed was known locally as Sureties' farm[38]. Apart from the marsh grazing land, it consisted mostly of garden ground. At the expiry of this lease, and consistently with the estate's normal practice, an advertisement appeared in the London press on December 2nd, 1785, inviting those wishing to tender for the whole or part to attend the charity trustees at the Aldgate schoolhouse on December 14th, and drawing attention to the feature that "Part of the said ground is well situated for building on". In 1783 the trustees had enfranchised the estate, and as freeholders they could now look for a longer letting. That they chose to do so indicates the laxity of their approach; a later generation was to criticise not only the failure to secure covenants which gave control over building operations - as to which there was by this time undoubtedly a good deal of experience in the central estates, not least in the City where the trustees worked and met - but the preference for long leases at all, over the temporary benefits available from rack-renting[39].

The successful applicant was William Gigney, a baker, of Well street, who offered a rent of £190 for a 61 year term, the 70 acres becoming known thereafter as Gigney's farm. His importance is that his holding extended to nearly three quarters of the entire East London estate of the charity. Disregarding so much as was within Bethnal Green parish - now part of Victoria Park - this amounts to nine tenths of the area of the estate situated in Hackney. So from 1786, for all practical purposes so long as the rent was paid, the trustees parted with the bulk of the northern and eastern part of their land, lying east of Well street and north of Well street common, stretching down to the boundary with Thomas Mann's land nearer Hackney Wick[40].

From the first, Gigney's aim was building development, on that part of the land near Well street that the lessors had already identified as suitable. But nothing in his arrangement with the trustees gave them any say in his dealings. Indeed it was experience of this lease in particular that gave a later generation of Cass trustees, like many another landlord, a firm appreciation of the need for a much closer control over lettings.

Like his ground landlords, Gigney could only respond to what the market wanted. There was a demand for large, grand houses with a pleasant outlook; there was equally a demand for groups of smaller houses for local workers and traders. Gigney aimed to meet both.

At the corner of Well street, where Cassland road now joins it, Gigney built on the east side a short row of small terraced houses, later to afford frontages for shops, which in the manner of many developers he called after himself: Gigney's place. (Again, fairly typically, this did not stick, as before long the terrace became known as Melville place.) His own baker's business may well have been transferred to this site, set back somewhat from the street at the back of a yard. In the under-leases he granted, Gigney was careful to protect his own business by providing that the tenant and any sub-tenant should refrain from carrying on any baker's business on their premises[41].

To the east he let land - 16 acres in all - to John Clark, who himself developed it in part, building a row of small houses, named in a similar way after their founder but later known as Nursery place. To the north, John Fletcher, a local gardener, sub-leased 2 acres, building himself the substantial villa that was later to become known as Grove cottage, and ultimately as "the Limes"; and developing land to the north in the form of a row of smaller tenements called Fletcher's gardens.

On the south side of the Common was built a group of 14 houses on which Gigney managed to put his stamp more effectively, as they were never known other than as Baker's row. Several of these, tiny and built back-to-back, were eventually taken by Leny Smith and Co. as housing for their workers at the Hackney Wick silk mills[42].

To fulfil his more grandiose plans, it was Gigney who first laid out the road that became Cassland road, on the line of an old track to the Wick. On the south side of this road, on the site of the present technical college, two plots were taken, and larger houses built than was the general tendency on Fletcher's and Clark's developments. One of the two plots went to Thomas Sell, a local flour factor. With financial help in the form of a mortgage from (presumably) a business associate, a Bermondsey pastrycook by the name of Wyatt, he built two houses fronting northwards onto the new road, selling both of them within a year to James Jackson, a City linen draper, for £400 and the discharge of Wyatt's mortgage. (They were substantially rebuilt by Jackson in the 1790's, and demolished in the 1840's to form the central site of the whole estate as the location of "Cassland house", the surveyor's residence and estate office). A further plot fronting Cassland road and adjacent to the original pair, set back from these and accessible by way of a narrow drive, was developed by one Thomas Smith at some time between 1794 and 1800, for the house which ultimately became known as "Terrace lodge"[43].

The second large plot was taken by Thomas Riddle, a gardener from Homerton. In 1787 he built a large and exceedingly plain mansion on the site of what is now Meynell gardens, overlooking the Common. The earliest name given to this building was "Common house".

To finance his road-building and other developments Gigney was borrowing extensively on mortgage. In addition to a handful of unlet houses "in carcase", by 1790 he still had some 42 acres (including much brickfield) in hand, this unrealised investment being valued in all (it seems optimistically) at some £186 annually. It is probable that he was involving himself as financier to the numerous speculators who took up the smaller plots of land on the triangular site east of Well street and north of the new road; the improved rental, above what he owed to the Cass trustees, must still have been insufficient to fund support of his sub-tenants' building. His own business

29

was also presumably in difficulties. Certainly by the summer of that year two of his creditors - a maltster and a timber merchant - decided that they could take no more: Gigney was bankrupt[44]. If, as is only too probable, he is the same William Gigney as is found a few years later operating as a chapman and general dealer near Bishopsgate, he had an unhappy end, quarrelsome and litigious[45].

James Jackson, the City linen-draper who had taken an assignment of Sell's plot, the larger of the two south of the new road, had seen the way things were going; on Gigney's bankruptcy he took the opportunity of straightening out his own tenure. In July 1790 he surrendered Sell's lease of the 2 acre site south of the road, obtaining a new lease of a slightly larger plot for the remaining 55 years of the original term, at a rent of £8 per year (which was favourable by comparison with Riddle's acre at 5 guineas, for example, or 4 acres further east let by the creditors at £20 annually).

The following February, Gigney's leasehold estate was put up for auction at the Green Dragon pub in Well street (which stood on the north side, near the Prior's house, more or less opposite the present junction with Cassland road). The auctioneer invited others to continue what Gigney had started, and to take advantage of his new road. The sale particulars included the following:

"Part of the above premises are most eligibly situate for Building, a Road being cut for that purpose from Well street to Hackney Wick, on each side of which a row of houses might be built so as to render it a very desirable Situation, and there being several Acres of excellent Brick Earth, with a Covenant for the Use of the same, on any Part of the Premises. Gentlemen in the Building Line will find it well worth their Attention."[46]

Hackney terrace

The building which in fact took place immediately following the sale of Gigney's lease and ground rents was not, however, on the land auctioned at the Green Dragon, but on the site that Jackson had secured for himself. The gentlemen who undertook the development were William Fellowes, a surveyor based in Southwark, and his two City partners, a plumber (John Shillitoe) and an attorney (Thomas Abree Pickering) who in July 1792 took a sub-underlease from James Jackson and, with his support, launched the building scheme that was to create Hackney terrace, the earliest of Hackney's few palace-front terraces and the most ambitious of its Georgian survivals[47].

The framework for their scheme was similar to that of the building societies which were beginning to form in the early 1790's, although the context was quite different from that of the typical building society. The mainstream of the building society movement was essentially working-class, being organised on the basis of weekly or fortnightly subscriptions of a few pence from working men, usually collected in a convenient pub, in return for which they would ultimately become entitled to own and occupy a freehold house. The earliest of these societies were to be found in the Midlands, rarely at that period in London, and it has been noted that so far there has been no building society of this period identified which was not associated with licensed premises[48].

Hackney terrace was designed to be more up-market. Nevertheless, the principle on which the three partners set up their project was very similar. Eighteen subscriptions were on offer. After four years, each subscriber was entitled, in return for his monthly subscription, to a lease, for the remainder of the developers' own term, of one house and one stable, to be allocated by ballot. (There was no mention of the manner of collection of the money, and certainly no identifiable hostelry[49].)

It was not the first such project with which this team had been involved. The previous year had seen the beginnings of a similar enterprise in Pollard's row, off the old Bethnal Green road, of which Fellowes was the architect and Shillitoe at the very least a builder and lessee. On a much larger scale (conceived, although almost certainly not fully implemented, as some 90 houses, in two sizes), this was also produced by monthly subscription. In such a side street a palace front, such as Hackney terrace was to have, would have been totally inappropriate. The front elevation featured, by way of decoration, only a plain projection of the brick doorcases and the grotesque animated keystones found elsewhere in the East End at the time[50]. Although the two-bay symmetry, ground floor string course and austere doorcase are entirely consistent with the architectural approach of Hackney terrace, the window apertures were of uniform size, and the ground floor was not raised, leaving the basement almost completely unlit from the front. Unlike that terrace, there was, however - as building society lore would dictate - a hostelry associated with the building: "Mr Baylis, White Hart, Bethnal Green Road, will shew the Ground". Indeed the development was marketed with a view to securing not only investors from the building trade, which would in the short term, help to accomplish the project in the trades which it currently lacked, but also shopkeepers who would, in settling on the development and (as invited) adapting their premises for business purposes, help to secure a viable community[51].

Fellowes and Shillitoe were themselves subscribers to the Pollard row enterprise; so far as is known Pickering was involved merely in a professional capacity[52]. In the Hackney terrace venture, begun at a time when the Pollard's row venture may have already run into trouble[53], all three took out subscriptions, and so did their immediate landlord, James Jackson. Subscriptions began (or so it was intended) in September 1792; each subscriber agreed to pay monthly until £252 had been handed over, and after that to be liable for an eighteenth share of the total cost of building (there was careful provision for an independent audit). The developers undertook that each house and stable should be worth £400.

Potential subscribers were shown front and rear elevations of a terrace of 18 houses, together with a similar number of stables, in a separate building lying to the south of the easternmost house's rear garden.

No express mention was made of gardens as such, but they were of the utmost importance to the developers' concept. There were to be not only the private back gardens (the terrace itself facing directly onto the road, in true urban fashion) but a communal "lawn", or "pleasure ground", accessible through gates from the back gardens and lying between them and the Common. Moreover, it seems to have become the developers' intention, if indeed it was not from the outset, to secure a garden prospect to the north also, by underleasing the land immediately opposite the site across the new road to the Wick, thereby preventing other gentlemen in the building line from obscuring the view sloping gently northwards across the fields to Morning lane[54].

The terrace as built is eloquent evidence of the developers' pride in their work; the three coats of arms featured in artificial stone on the pediment are those, reading from east to west, of Fellowes, Shillitoe and Pickering.

There can be no doubt that of the three William Fellowes was responsible for the design, which appears in the result to owe a good deal to the type of terrace epitomised in Bedford square and favoured in the early 1790's in other developing suburbs south of the river, such as Surrey square, Walworth and Gloucester crescent, Greenwich (these being by another more famous Southwark architect, Michael Searles). It does not however feature amongst the handful of designs Fellowes exhibited at the Royal Academy. (It was only near his death, in 1816, that Fellowes was prepared to describe himself as an architect.)[55]

No doubt, equally, the enterprise benefited from Shillitoe contributing the expertise of his trade - his coat of arms has pride of place on the pediment - and Pickering was presumably responsible for, if not necessarily the originator of, the legal structure of the arrangement, which was at the least unorthodox for a middle class development. There seems, as in Pollard row, to have been a deliberate attempt to involve a range of different trades, although there was, with only eighteen houses, less scope for a wide spectrum, whether of specialists or social strata; and indeed the eighteen resulting underleases came into only a few hands.

The short-term profit element for the developers was to have been in this underlease (the fourth in the chain of leases, starting with that of Gigney's creditors) which they undertook to grant to subscribers in the autumn of 1796, four years from the beginning of the enterprise. Each house was to yield a ground rent of £3. 13s. 6d (£3.66) annually; the developers reserved to themselves any benefit they could obtain by finishing the houses early and letting them at a rack rent. As it happened this last was a pious hope. No doubt the progress of works was affected by the local and national downward trend in the building and building supply market after 1792.

By the time the first leases were due to be granted in 1796 only 10 houses were finished. Only 8 houses were occupied in 1797; it seems to have been 1801 before all were occupied[56].

The first lessees, other than the three progenitors of the project and the ground landlord Jackson, were James Adey, a sash-frame maker (nos. 6 and 16), Samuel

Ireland, a stonemason (nos. 4 and 11); Thomas Baily, an ironmonger (nos. 3 and 17); and William Bottomley, a carpenter (nos. 2, 7, 13, and 15)[57].

The financial arrangements between the subscribers involved, in some cases, considerable complexity. There must also have been some departure from the original design for the rear elevation, although whether the more striking version for nos. 5 to 18 (which features a semicircular bow over three or in one case four storeys) was the original or an afterthought it is not possible now to be certain. Another departure from the original plan involved the stables, which lay to the east of the Lawn; it is not clear that the full 16 were ever built, and some houses were leased without a stable, whereas Jackson took more than the number to which the number of his leases would, on the assumptions of the original articles of agreement, have entitled him.

Pickering's own financial transactions were complex, and included lending on mortgage to Bottomley, the Bermondsey carpenter who had evidently got into difficulties. The three partners had themselves raised capital from Pickering's family, £800 at the outset and again at the four year point.

At this time, when the three principals, under whatever form of mutual arrangement was by then in force, were ready to subscribe for leases to individual houses, the end of the partnership was signalled by partitioning, in what seem to be unequal shares, another parcel of land, opposite the terrace, which they had bought from Gigney's successor. No doubt, as was also the case between the three and the builders, account had at this stage to be taken of who had contributed what to the enterprise. It was this land, nevertheless, the bulk of which was never further developed, that secured the open prospect to the north, and settled the expectation that in front of the terrace there should be gardens, not houses. If there had ever been any intention of building on this land it was abandoned.

It has been suggested elsewhere[58] that Fellowes, once he had prepared the plans and elevation, took little interest in the execution of the interiors, whose asymmetry contradicts the extreme care taken in the design of the facade, and in the preparation of the leases, which prohibited changes to the fronts of the houses other than the addition of balconies. Individual houses demonstrate internal variations, presumably to suit the preferences of their first lessees or occupiers, particularly on the second storey, which may be divided into three or occasionally two rooms; and in the basement, which may or may not have originally had rear access at this level. (Other variations came later, with the addition, in the 1840's onwards, of small rear extensions to afford internal W.C.s.).

Leaving aside the reversed staircases and attenuated bows of the back elevations at the western end, there were a range of different fireplace and rear window designs, although the woodwork and plain cornice work in the entrance hall was standard. Only a handful of balconies appeared, these being the only variation to the original elevation that the developers' lease permitted. On the whole the simplicity of the internal detail mirrors the austerity of the facade.

Each house was provided with a water supply, in the form of a well (a circular brick chamber about eight feet in diameter) shared with its immediate neighbour. These nine wells were situated some ten feet from the rear wall of each house, below the brick walls of the long back gardens and bisected by the line of these walls. These, as previously mentioned, opened into an enclosed communal garden, the lawn, or pleasure ground, which in turn opened on to Well street Common. This garden, laid out as a central lawn with shrub beds around the perimeter, was, in a thoroughly modern fashion, run democratically by the tenants, each of whom was entitled to call a meeting of all eighteen to discuss and regulate its management by leaving a "summons" at each house and giving six days' notice.

Completion by subscribers would, arguably, entitle Hackney terrace to be considered as among the earliest, if not the very earliest, surviving development by a building society, being both started and finished before the first known development by a conventional society run along subscription lines: Club row, Longridge, near Preston in Lancashire[59]. However, in addition to the differences noted earlier, it is atypical of the conventional building society, in being built for revenue or investment rather than for occupation by its developers.

There is one reservation on this point, however. Equally untypically of London palace terraces, Hackney terrace was indeed intended, by one of its developers at any rate, for owner-occupation. Although none of the others went into residence (they all owned underleases, at least one of these being retained by the family throughout its term), Thomas Pickering lived in the Terrace (at number 8, although he also owned 14) for upwards of 30 years, retaining his attorney's practice in Lincoln's Inn while from his terrace address championing the rights of commoners of Hackney against the parish authorities and the manor steward[60]. Here, one may suppose, was the prime mover of Hackney terrace, who in Pollard's row had seen the device for enabling himself and others of like mind to escape from the City filth to a life among gardens and fields. In doing so he brought with him a quintessentially urban architecture, that to this day stands out amidst the suburban style of the neighbouring buildings of some sixty and more years later almost as starkly as it must once have stood out amongst the busy countryside.

Part Two: The Framework for 19th Century Development

The influence of the Park

The Cass trustees, when in the 1840's they came to assess the prospects for redevelopment on the expiry of the Gigney lease of 1786, found themselves unhappy with the standard of the later building on the eastern part of this land, particularly the shanties of "Hackney Bay", allegedly by association with the criminality of Botany bay, on the eastern part of what was later called Cassland road[61]. Other developments in Grove street and Well street can have been no more pleasing.

The most significant, and infinitely more auspicious, development was however the decision of the Government not only to build Victoria Park, but to build it on the northern of two alternative sites, lying eastwards of Bonner's fields, Bethnal Green, and consisting of market gardens, grazing and arable land in equal proportions.

The decision resulted from the perception that for crowded and underprivileged East London (some 30,000 of whose residents had in 1840 petitioned the Queen for a Royal Park in their neighbourhood) such provision was not only an amenity but a necessity; in 1839 the Registrar General had drawn attention to the significantly higher mortality in east as compared with west London. Once the idea had been conceived, it was followed by the further aim of "improving the neighbourhood" by the building of substantial middle class houses, leading to some recovery of the outlay involved. The initial cost was, in part at any rate, to be met by the sale of York House, St James's (now Lancaster House), which had come into Government hands as a result of the bankruptcy of George III's second son, the "Grand Old Duke of York" of the nursery rhyme.

James Pennethorne, surveyor to the Crown estate, would have preferred a site around Bow Common lane; his view was that the northern site was flat and dull, and that development of water resources for recreation and for building land was made very expensive by the nature of the soil. He considered that the Bow Common site would be cheaper to develop in the long run, and that the improvement of the area generally would be enhanced by the fact that the tanning, blood-boiling and other noxious activities then carried out in that area would be driven out. The Commissioners of Woods and Forests, however, preferred the 237 acres of the more northerly site, straddling the boundaries of Bethnal Green, Hackney and Bow, on the grounds that the cost was just over half of Pennethorne's preferred southern site. This ignored the recognised fact that estimated development costs were greater, and that more expensive access roads would be required. The short term cost was, however, more convenient to Government; and it has been suggested that the elimination of

Bonner's fields as a resort for disorderly gatherings was a factor in the choice[62].

Plans were drawn up swiftly, and a Bill presented to Parliament. The Commissioners took powers to lease up to one quarter of the site to be acquired for the building of houses, and Pennethorne drew up a site plan showing suitably large, detached villas in substantial grounds, both on the north and on the south sides of the proposed Park, with ornamental buildings, lodges and outbuildings[63].

The proposals involved the acquisition of substantial tracts of land belonging to the Cass trustees and to the Governors of St Thomas's hospital, as well as part of that of Captain Sotheby, the Three Colts tavern and tea garden and (in the north-eastern part of the site) the entire local estate of the late William Thompson of Stamford Hill. The Thompson, Cass and St Thomas's holdings were readily acquired, but numerous other landowners (including the landlord of the Three Colts, and the owners of Sir George Duckett's canal) held out for more than the Commissioners were prepared to pay, prolonging the negotiations and subsequent arbitration for over five years.

Some of the market gardeners' houses were retained, the only one now surviving (others having been destroyed by enemy action during the last war) being the White Lodge facing Homer road, which is probably the house built by or for the market gardener Alexander Leighton on Thompson's land under an agreement of 1837[64]. The only remaining buildings by the Commissioners themselves from the Park's early days are the three keepers' lodges of 1857, designed in the Office of Works by John Phipps[65].

Nevertheless, by 1845, still incomplete, the Park was in use. Public order was a problem in the early days; it seems that the public sought access and took matters into their own hands before the authorities were properly prepared for them. Some 700 fruit trees, whose presence was thought to "induce disorder", were removed, to be replaced by over 4,000 evergreen and deciduous trees, and 1,000 shrubs[66].

Numerous activities such as preaching (eventually banned after "unbecoming scenes"), military bands and an increasing volume of public meetings gradually diminished the revenue the Commissioners could expect from letting on grazing tenancies (although sheep continued to grace the Park until well into this century). Water was originally introduced partly for their benefit, despite misgivings that the likely popularity of bathing facilities would harm the eventual value of the intended building development.

Pennethorne's original plan for Grove road, that it should be sunk and its sides embanked to lessen its impact on the overall design, was never implemented.

The Commissioners' plans for impressive villa development, on the model of Regent's Park, did not take off; early advertisements for villa sites found no response at all.

The stickiness of the market could scarcely be lost on others with an interest in estate development in the neighbourhood. In October 1851, George Wales, surveyor to the Cass estate, quite reasonably saw the future of his employers' estate as inextricably bound up with the Park; and, being the man he was, did not hesitate to make his views known to the Crown authorities, in a characteristically forceful letter of October 1851:

"The Sir John Cass trustees have expended such a large amount on the formation of roads etc. for the improvement of their Estate (which forms almost the entire northern boundary of the Park, exceeding a mile in length) that they feel they have some claim in pressing this question -

Since 1844 they have been diligently labouring and hoping from year to year that the approaches would be made -

Your Architect Mr Pennethorne will I believe speak favourably of all the operations I have carried out, and will not hesitate to confess that Sir John Cass's estate will now greatly assist the Park, whereas in 1844 there was every reason to apprehend some prejudice.

As a Resident in the locality, I can speak confidently that public expectation as to the approaches to the Park and the letting of the Building land is certainly falling - respectable men (inclined generally to look on the bright side) constantly express their opinion that the approaches never will be made and that the land will never let - this assertion has some force remembering that the Park has been formed more than 10 years, and the Parliamentary notices for the approaches given 3 times, and yet there is not a fair travelling way to the Park..."[67]

Public expectation was more than justified. The Crown estate had had large expectations of establishing a solid, fashionable middle-class suburb around the Park, and laid out Approach road in Bethnal Green with this in mind, based on no greater evidence than the theory of so many London estates that once houses were built the appropriate class of tenant would queue up to take leases. Far from this being the outcome, in fact there were scarcely any builders prepared to build. A minor building lease was granted in 1851 for two houses in Old Ford Road, and then in 1856 the London Chest Hospital was built on the south side of the Park.

Indeed as early as 1852 the Commissioners seem to have realised that there would be no pressure on building land, as the Act of that year defined for building a much reduced area on the perimeter, closer to a sixth than the quarter originally permitted. It was not until 1854, just as several lean building years were beginning, that Pennethorne was asked to draw up a layout for building on the Hackney side; and it was 1860 before the first lease was granted[68].

Wales, however, was most concerned about the southern approaches. (He was not alone in this; Hackney vestry itself sent a deputation to the Commissioners to press for progress.) His estate plan of 1850 shows the proposed south-western extension of Approach road, which would, if it had ever been built, have cut through the present gardens at Bethnal Green to form the better link with the City which it was thought was essential to a successful building estate on either side of the Park. It was this to which he was referring in his plea to the Commissioners[69].

The Commissioners being unable to fund the roads which might have made their building projects more desirable (projects which, in their turn, might have provided the money for the roads) the Cass estate and the other South Hackney estates who were contemplating development were faced with optimising the internal layout of the area, accessible either through the Park on Grove road, or from Mare street at Cambridge Heath or Well street. The intended south- western approach, extending Approach Road itself, was indeed never built, but Burdett road was eventually laid out by the Metropolitan Board of Works in 1862, thus completing in so far as it ever would be completed the access to the Park. Thus the additional access eventually provided was not for the City clientele the Cass estate would have wished, but for the benefit of the inhabitants of the riverside settlements of its intended catchment area, and named to honour the Baroness Burdett Coutts, one of the Park's benefactors in the form of the elaborate Gothic drinking fountain in the eastern section.

The fact that for much of its length the southern boundary of the Park has been Sir George Duckett's - now the Hertford Union - canal can have been only beneficial to the South Hackney estates. The north bank remained protected from the infiltration of the small industrial premises that otherwise could well have encroached beyond their foothold along the Regent's canal between Limehouse and Bow, as far north as the rear of the Crown Hotel in Grove road.

The Superintendent's Lodge, South West Entrance, Victoria Park

Co-operation between estate owners

Where long leases for building or merely for management had been granted by different landowners in the area, it is noticeable that they tended to fall in within the same decade. Thus the leases granted by St Thomas's and the Cass trustees in the 1780's all came to an end in the 1840's. The other large estate, that of the Norris family, had during the tenure of Henry Handley Norris (who inherited in 1803) been, in the language of our own time, owner-occupied, and hence was able to respond flexibly to whatever local pressures for development might come to bear.

While this coincidence in dates and periods may be no more than the result of identical economic pressures producing similar and contemporary responses, landowners were also well aware that it was in their mutual interest to co-operate over development plans. This took several forms.

Primarily they co-operated on the alignment of roads through the estates. The Parr estate, Hedger's and those of Mann and Mills were either too small, too isolated or both to participate in the schemes of the larger landowners. The latter, however, by developing long, broad thoroughfares, each of which traversed at least one estate boundary, were able to plan housing of a more prestigious kind than would have been possible on a series of smaller estates each enclosed on itself.

Victoria Park road as originally conceived (that is to say the western arm, between Cambridge Heath and the Lauriston road roundabout, the eastern stretch being known as Grove street lane or road and then, briefly and confusingly, as Wick lane) was designed to form the boundary between the Cass estate and Norris estate on the north, and the Crown estate on the south. Where straight alignment produced a pepperpotting of small isolated parcels of land detached from the main estate, suitable exchange often proved quite simple to arrange (if sometimes the arranging was rather prolonged: as St Thomas's and Cass were both charitable estates any deal by either had to go under the scrutiny of the Charity Commissioners, and Norris took his time until the moment suited his purposes).

Thus the site of the Alexandra pub, anciently an isolated field belonging to the Norris family and on account of its isolation let for long periods to the tenants of neighbouring Cass property, was finally absorbed into the Cass holdings. Its transfer, in exchange for a parcel on the north side of Victoria park road which enabled the Norris estate eventually to create a sensible north-south alignment of Handley road, ended over a century of contention over rights of way and drainage consequent on consistent common tenancy by neighbouring Cass lessees[70]. Equally, the site for the present nos. 57 to 83 (and the former 53-5, "Harley villas") were acquired by Cass from the Crown, in exchange for a narrow strip running west from the southern limb of Skipworth road[71]. (In recent years Cass estate management policy has led to a considerable portion of the north of Victoria Park road being returned to the Crown estate.)

ST JOHN'S TERRACE.

St John's Terrace, Lauriston road, drawn by Samuel Parr

The pre-development Shore road petered out south of the ancient house of Shore place into a footpath towards the canal; this path traversed both the St Thomas and Cass estates and readily lent itself to replacement by a wide road linking Well street to the new Victoria Park road. St Thomas's road (the northern end now being Ainsworth and the southern Skipworth road) was however an artificial creation arising out of co-operation by both estates[72].

Fremont and Warneford streets, built on the Hickling estate, would have been without their access to Victoria Park road (ironically all too successful, as now subject to traffic restrictions) but for a deal struck between the Cass and the Hickling trustees in 1851, with the co-operation of the Crown Commissioners, whereby a small triangle of land at the extreme south-eastern corner of the Hickling estate was conveyed to Cass in return for the latter's agreeing to construct a road on it - and by inference their own adjoining land. What Cass gained by this was a modicum of extra building frontage, founding the opportunity for increased ground rents from the plot for a pair of semi-detached villas, spacious as any on the estate, taken for building on the west

40

corner the following year by J A Hughes; and eventually from Harley villas, tucked in behind Gordon villas (nos. 57-67) in the 1860's[73].

Other exchanges to effect alignment of the Cass boundaries took place with the Hedger estate at Hackney Wick and with Poole's charity estate, to enable coherent development at Terrace road and Queen Anne road[74]. There was also the need for alignment between St Thomas's and the Norris estate, which led not only to a suitable layout at Speldhurst road (St Thomas's property lying to the west and Norris's to the east) but to a mutually satisfactory approach to the main roads on each estate, which made possible a wider, grander King Edward's road, and one which offered on approach from the west a handsome prospect of the west front of the new church of St John of Jerusalem[75].

This instance of co-operation between the two estate owners had a feature of particular interest. In 1845, when Henry Currey, first of a dynasty of surveyors to St Thomas's hospital, was commissioned to draw up a road scheme for its South Hackney estate, the neighbouring Norrises had no intention of building immediately. Henry Norris V, resident in Oxfordshire and without any intention of returning to Hackney, had been managing his father's Hackney estate since 1843. In 1850, shortly before the death of H. H. Norris, both estates commissioned the same surveyor to devise complementary schemes for each, so that the precise alignment of King Edward's road - originally conceived in mid-decade - would benefit both estates.

That the Norris family had no serious intention of building - on the estate as a whole at any rate - is clear from the fact that the design east of Lauriston road trails off well short of the estate boundary, and indeed the ovals and circuses shown suggest that the surveyor may have been having a little illustrative fun rather than creating a serious building plan.

On the other hand, an approach by the Cass trustees to the Frampton executors, when their estate north of Well street was being planned, came to nothing; indeed there was no common boundary, and the Cass perception that a high class of property on Frampton land, linked by a wide road cut through the intervening cluster of building to the rear of the Prior's house, would suit their own purposes may well not have recommended itself to the other side. In the same way, an approach by Marmaduke Matthews for access to his Wick road land was initially stalled by the Cass trustees, but seems to have led ultimately to Union, now Bradstock, road providing a link between the two estates[76].

A further approach by George Wales, this time to the Crown estate in April 1855, was prompted by Pennethorne's original plan to effect the north-westerly exit to the Park well out of alignment with what was perceived to be the approach to it through both the St Thomas's and Cass estates, down Shore road and St Agnes's terrace. Pennethorne readily recommended his masters to agree to a change, as producing all round a better effect and greater convenience[77], although as Shore road remained out of exact alignment the change was not as radical as Wales might have wished.

Perhaps more than any other single factor it was this recognition of inter-dependence between the various landed interests that leads to the difficulty, post-development, of identifying even 18th century field boundaries on the ground in South Hackney, other than on the very smallest estates or the outer edges of the larger. The Mann estate at Hackney Wick, so far as its eastern and western boundaries are concerned, represents a field identifiable on Rocque's map, as do the rear boundaries of Warneford and Fremont streets and Balcorne street (notably the curious rear boundary of the Clarendon Arms). Otherwise, there was a good deal of rationalisation at the edges of the larger estates, and post war redevelopment has overlaid these in any event. Even Meynell crescent, the last 19th century development on any scale in South Hackney, smoothed out the edge of the common field.

The System of Building Leases
The eight functions

In Hackney, it was the middle of the 19th century before the system of building leases, which had been evolving in central London at least since the mid-17th century, had its full effect on development.

This system would commonly involve as many as eight different roles or functions, from ground landlord to ultimate occupier, in the production of a house - perhaps more than eight, if journeymen builders working for one another on a sub-contracting basis are counted in.

First in the chain are the ground landlords,who had the advantage of having land developed systematically, without necessarily incurring any expenditure themselves. The leasehold system would give them unencumbered title to the developed property on the expiry of the lease. The builder or speculator would, on account of his commitment, pay a ground rent less than a full rack rent; it would fall to him, as he had undertaken to repair the house during the term of the lease and to deliver it up in good condition, to let it by the month or the year for whatever rack rent the market would bear, for as long as the lease ran. The builder's reduced ground rent to the freeholder would however be a great deal higher than a farmer or market gardener would pay, pro rata, for the same piece of ground.

The system held the greatest appeal, of course, for those landowners whose family or other financial interests moved them to look some way into the future. Below a certain size of estate the dynastic impulse might not seem worth indulging: John Parr's family did not hesitate to sell freehold of part of his five acres or so if a suitable offer materialised, but to develop on a leasehold basis would have been natural to Henry Norris V, sole heir to Henry Handley Norris, who also had estate elsewhere to assist in securing the future of his two sons and four daughters.

The corporate, charitable landowners had no choice, being prohibited by law from alienating their endowment. Even to grant a building lease was hazardous, as the arrangement might be upset if found to be not to the best advantage of the beneficiaries of the charity. Their natural course, in the interests of maximum revenue, if the property had got beyond the point when a repairing lease was a marketable proposition, was to rack rent existing buildings for as long their state of repair warranted it.

Thus charities' building leases are not often found before the passing of the Charitable Trusts Act 1853, which enabled some security to attach to such arrangements, by empowering the Charity Commissioners to sanction not only building leases themselves but the demolition of property, where this was an essential preliminary to redevelopment. They might also consent to its total alienation, but this was such a hazardous procedure as to prove at times a complete deterrent to a prospective purchaser, even one itself a charity.

In South Hackney, where much land was held by copy of court roll (copyhold) from the Lord of the Manor (the manor in question being principally that of Lordshold, and the Lord the head for the time being of the Tyssen family), it was necessary to enfranchise the land before development, as without obtaining the freehold in this way development was in the gift of the manorial court, the procedure for granting leases cumbersome, expensive and anachronistic, to say nothing of the leases themselves being for a maximum of 31 years, unattractively short for investment from the point of view either of the speculator or the landowner intent on securing sound building practice.

The freeholder intending development - or indeed the long leaseholder, such as James Jackson of Hackney terrace, who might himself be tempted by an increased rental for the remainder of his term - might expect himself to meet the initial costs of basic essentials such as road layout and sewerage, or to leave this to the individual forming the second link in the chain, a speculator, who would incur, or pass on, the risks of putting up houses and making up the necessary roads, often by extending his credit with a third, the supplier of building materials. (This third individual was unlikely to become involved in the building process directly, unless the speculator got into difficulties, when he might himself have to step in and realise his defaulting debtor's assets - this was of course what had happened when the timber merchant Jeremiah Blakeman blew the whistle on William Gigney's activities; or he chose as developer to take leases in hand, as did T. F. Kelly in Victoria park road, and the Winkley brothers in Meynell crescent[78].

In the 18th century the arrangement might be a straightforward one such as Thomas Flight's with the Governors of St Thomas's Hospital, where the consideration for the lease was Flight's undertaking to spend a large sum in putting up houses. This gave the freeholder little or no control over what was in fact done on the land, and a great deal of trouble and expense might be occasioned (although in this case no problem seems to have occurred) if the covenants were not performed. (In this instance, for example, there was no qualification on the tenant's option to renew.) In its more developed form, the arrangement characteristically took the form of a building agreement, whereby the speculator agreed to put up one, or two, or four, or a hundred and fifty houses, and would become entitled to a lease of each house or group of houses (often in twos or fours) as the carcases were completed and roofed, with materials and to a standard satisfactory to the landowner. In the meantime he would expect a trivial or even a notional rent to be payable, if demanded, such as the legendary peppercorn.

In large transactions, such as those for Harrowgate road or for Annis and Christie roads, the arrangement which was ultimately evolved, largely as a product of experience of unfulfilled agreements, might be that a handful of houses would be kept back from the developer until all were completed, and that letting was in any event dependent on a certain rate of progress each year[79]. The later equivalent of Flight's covenant for expenditure was the covenant, equally intractable in enforcement if for different reasons, that the building would generate a minimum level of income; such as Borton's undertaking that the annual value of houses built on his Cass land south of Victoria Park road would be not less than £24 annually[80].

The speculator would probably need, fourth, a surveyor or architect, to draw up the plans and elevations. From an early date, however, this might be the most dispensable of all the functions, because there would be numerous pattern books available, giving elevations and specifications for houses of all sizes and pretensions in whatever style was fashionable, to which patterns only a little elegant individualisation might be sought by builder or tenant - or, if the speculator was in luck, might not.

He would, unless of extensive means himself, certainly need, fifth, a financier. Before mid-century this would usually be a private individual, perhaps introduced by his solicitor (and sometimes a member of the solicitor's family) who was looking for an investment, secured by a mortgage and "as safe as houses". By this means he might find a small occasional investor - say a widow from a country town or quiet suburb with a few hundred pounds to invest; or something more systematic, where a wealthy individual with a West End address would be happy to continue, over a period of years, to back a developer he trusted to put up sound, readily marketable houses.

Thus the builder William Norris - no relation, confusingly enough, of the landowning family - who was active in Hackney from the 1840's onwards, had his own tame investor, John Chave Luxmoore, who might also sponsor his subcontractors; although he was not a stranger to building societies when suitable[81]. Hugh Eastman, active in the 1860's, tended to be sponsored by one or other of the Sheffield family, City solicitors (with relatives in the business of building supply) who had lived for a time in one of the houses to the west of Hackney terrace, Eastman's own residence for a short time[82].

Charles Butters worked largely in tandem with T. P. Glaskin, a financier who blurred the edges of the functions further by apparently taking on the developer's role as well, taking such a close interest in each development that his own residence moved from one to another, in the manner of many developer/builders.

Less frequent, but far from unknown, was the situation where City merchants risked their own capital in building ventures: it seems that what survives of Bentham road and the entire Frampton estate, among others, were financed in this way, by the Innes brothers and T. P. Glaskin respectively, as there is no record of mortgages on these properties by these speculators. (It is curious to note that a number of South Hackney developer-financiers, notably Glaskin, Thomas Kelsey and Hamilton of Shore place, had made their money in the wholesale textile business.) The Innes brothers, who took leases for the south side of Bentham road, saw themselves merely as "wholesalers" in land. And towards mid-century, mortgages from building societies became commoner, to the point where this became easily the most frequent method of financing house-building, the finance being made available not, as now, to the owner-occupier (who then very rarely had any stake in the house longer than an annual lease) but to the builder or speculator on the security of his building. It might be easier for a non-established figure such as Henry Bagge to raise finance in this relatively impersonalised way.

Very occasionally, participation in the so-called "Starr Bowkett" form of building society, where entitlement to borrow on mortgage depended to some extent on a lottery, might enable a journeyman builder himself to enter the market as a speculator on a small scale. Such was the means whereby E. C. Newman part-financed a development of six houses, sub-contracted from Henry Bagge, in Harrowgate road[83].

The finance arranged, then came the need for the sixth function, that of a competent master builder, who would take charge of the actual construction, and of hiring (if the necessary trades were not to be found amongst such employees as he might have) seventh, sub-contracting journeymen builders and craftsmen of the bricklaying, plastering, plumbing, and woodworking trades. Obviously a large-scale agreement would require sub-contracting on a commensurately large scale: there is no evidence that the South Hackney builders retained large workforces[84].

At this point the leasing arrangements might take on considerable complexity. Supposing the original speculator to have had an agreement with the ground landlord that on a particular plot he would build, say, 150 houses (as in 1864 John Wright agreed with the Cass trustees that he would do, in what became Annis and Christie roads). He would need, to fulfil the agreement within a stipulated time (three years in this case) to engage several master craftsmen to carry out the work, without which the landlords would not, at the stipulated time (almost always when the house was roofed in and completed "in carcase", without necessarily being finished as to the interior) grant him the lease he would then be entitled to. Thus John Wright's development of 1864 involved at least seven master builders taking each between 4 and 10 houses in each subordinate agreement, the main sub-contractors being R. T. Banks of Dagmar terrace, who was responsible for at least 24, and William Tully of Dagmar road, with at least 25. One of Wright's sub-contractors, Evan Lewis, was himself the main contractor for Kenton cottages on the west side of Kenton road[85].

In return for labour and expense, he might direct the landlord, when the time came, to execute the lease in favour of such a sub-contractor, or indeed of a nominee of his, who might be either of the characters representing the eighth function, the consumer of the finished product. This would be either an investor in houses - a moneyed individual, legatee or even small-scale speculator (such perhaps as George Webb, butcher in Curtain road, Shoreditch, who invested heavily in terraced houses in Cassland road in the 1860's; or the tragic protagonist of Arthur Morrison's story "All that Messuage") - or, should the builder decide to perform that function himself, the householder him or herself, who would take either a monthly or an annual lease from the investor.

Equally, the speculator might take the lease himself, and sub-let, at a higher rent, either to one of his builders or to one of the other people who formed links in this extended chain, with a view either to building up a portfolio himself, or selling it on as a going concern to fund some future speculation; or he might, more commonly, assign his lease for a premium and plough the proceeds back into another project.

Shortening the chain

It would however be far from exceptional for there to be several fewer links in the chain between landlord and ultimate tenant; some individuals would combine several of the functions themselves. Thus Samuel Parr, second in his family to be landowner in Holcroft road and Balcorne street, was himself a surveyor by profession, and probably also financed development by his master builder William Turner. Marmaduke Matthews, an auctineer and surveyor, not only developed part of Wick road but sold off much of the grounds of his own house (on the site of St Joseph's Hospice) for housing and a chapel.

The master builder of sufficient standing could himself stand in the developer's shoes, once he had sufficient credibility to persuade a mortgagee that he was a good risk. There are several instances of this in South Hackney, one being William Norris, and another Henry Bagge, who is first met around 1860 as a master craftsman (he was a bricklayer by trade), in other words fulfilling the seventh function in the process, putting up individual houses on the Frampton estate, working to the master builder Charles Butters and his developer, T. P. Glaskin. By 1862, Bagge had himself, with Robert Morley, carpenter and fellow Frampton builder, entered into a building agreement with the landowner Henry Norris V for laying out the whole of the western part of the Norris estate and the eastern frontage of Lauriston road, and subsequently Bagge alone went on to develop Harrowgate road on a similar basis for the Cass trustees[86].

46

A building tradesman might, where the scale of the development was small, fill all the roles (other than that of providing the finance) between developer and occupier, and invest in a neighbouring house or two to boot. Thus Robert Kitteridge, a carpenter of Well street, in 1857 built and leased 2 houses (now 18 and 20) in Kenton road from the Cass trustees, and apparently retained them, using the back land as his builder's yard[87].

Many other builders moved in to their own houses, the better, presumably to supervise remaining works. (One can only imagine that in some cases it may have taken a very thick skin to do so, with the ultimate consumers as near neighbours.) John Page (who laid out Elsdale street in the early 1850's, the first development under the control, properly so called, of the Cass trustees) was the first of many, having come east from Barnsbury to do so. Others were Hugh Eastman, in 71 Victoria Park road ("Eastbourne House",1861), and T. P. Glaskin, an early resident on the second phase of development of Shore road, in number 26 (1856). But all of these, like many before and since, moved on when their local development was complete and other, greater prospects beckoned.

Eastman illustrates a further combination of roles. Originally he described himself as a "merchant" or even "iron agent", when from his base at East villa, Navarino road, he took leases - in the speculator/developer's role - from the Cass trustees of his first developments in Victoria Park road. It is however evident from his subsequent career that he had other ideas. By the late 1860's, having laid out a sizable chunk of the north side of Victoria Park road - most of it, fortunately, surviving - he is found in business as a surveyor, with offices in Gracechurch street; a few years later, he describes himself as "architect and surveyor", no less. He therefore functions as developer, architect, investor and occupier of Eastbourne house, and as the first three in relation to many others[88].

George Wales, another surveyor by profession who functioned also as an architect, demonstrates a similar versatility. He was surveyor to the Cass estate, and appears to have designed, or at any rate supervised the design of, numerous buildings on the Cass and other estates, demonstrating a range of styles which prove that he, at least, could go beyond the pattern books. He or his family also funded one or two small scale developments, by Page and others, around Well street and Cassland road, and took a leading role in the rebuilding of the north side of Church crescent. A good deal of the visual quality of what remains of mid-19th century South Hackney is owed to this one man.

The building lease

It has already been noted that the obligations placed on Thomas Flight in his building lease for Shore place in 1768 left him under scarcely any enforceable constraint. Other than standard covenants as to rent, and to deliver the demised premises up in repair (loosely expressed, as the premises were expressed to include

"Shoreditch place otherwise Shore House...now occupied by Nehemiah King", which Flight appears to have demolished immediately on the grant of the lease) Flight's only positive obligation was to build 5 or 6 new tenements for an outlay of £6,000. Had he failed to do so, the Governors of St Thomas's Hospital could have been faced with elaborate legal proceedings to forfeit his lease, whose outcome may have been uncertain, or (supposing he met the rent in the meantime) denying his entitlement to extend the period for a further 21 years, an option which he exercised in 1792 by directing a new lease of the land, part to himself and part to his sub-tenant Gedaliah Gatfield.

The Flight lease was in its looseness not dissimilar to the Cass lease to Gigney. By 1845, when planning for repossession of this sizable portion of their holding, the Cass trustees resolved never again to permit letting without taking greater control of underletting: although the more developed form of building lease which they began to employ was designed to ensure enhanced building standards before the ultimate lease was granted, as a condition of its grant.

This evolved, more or less, through trial and error. In the 1850's the estate developed a standard form of building proposal, ultimately in a printed pro forma, which the prospective builder (probably with the surveying office's help), filled in, altering it as he saw fit. The signed proposal, when accepted by the trustees, was follwed by a formal building agreement (originally a lease, but later an agreement to take a lease in an agreed form) whose execution would entitle the builder to the grant of (usually) an 80 year lease, sometimes, and increasingly so towards to the end of the century, to 90 years' enjoyment of the property improved with his labour and expense.

Thus a great deal turned on the detail of this proposal, as well as the form of the eventual lease. The Cass trustees were anxious to take tighter control of underletting than they had done hitherto: but there were other lessons that remained to be learnt. A control over underletting did not contemplate a control over unauthorised building, and so the assignee of 6-10 Cassland road could not effectively be prevented from putting up three tiny cottages on the Grove street frontage at the rear. Equally, a dispute between John Page and the estate as to the covenants to be included in the lease had to be resolved according to the terms of their original dealings[89].

The developed form of building agreement included not only detailed specification as to type and standard of the essential materials, but directions for compliance with the instructions of the estate surveyor.

Even this developed form made unstated assumptions which its acceptance later exposed when they proved to be unwarranted. In the early days of the estate's active building period, it is likely that the estate surveyor was himself the architect of much of the building constructed, and so there was relatively little chance that the design produced by an accepted proposal would be unacceptable to the owners - what chance there was would depend on a proposer's market, although even then the surveyor would be able to comment adversely on a design, as George Wales did with his fellow-surveyor James Lovegrove's design for Fern villas in Victoria Park road.

Although it was the estate's standard practice to stipulate, where possible, that the builder should make up the roads and kerbing, and pay a contribution, on granting of the lease, towards the provision of sewerage, only the latter formed part of the printed pro forma, and the former was left, somewhat surprisingly, to be inserted in some form such as a special condition to the effect that the builder was "to form the intended road to the satisfaction of the Surveyor..." As road-making might well be left until substantial numbers of leases had been granted this was a fruitful area for dispute with builders. Furthermore Wales's successor observed that the standard form of proposal was as often as not substantially varied in practice, although it may be that this was as much the result of a broad discretion in design being left to the surveyor as otherwise[90].

To a large extent the estate owners were in the hands of the builders themselves, who would only build what they would build and where they would build it. Edwards' insistence, when he put in for the first substantial plot (nos. 3 to 8) in Queen Anne Road, that he would not build half-basements, then (1865) beginning to become unfashionable, appears to have been accepted with hesitation and reluctance, no doubt because the estate wanted to push yet further east the larger type of villas built in Cassland crescent and road. Accepted, however, it was[91].

The Cass estate continued to be pragmatic about variations from the original proposal. Bishop's offer, in June 1865, to build the later, eastern segment of Cassland crescent on a design to match the western part of some ten years earlier was readily varied on his subsequent request not only to change the elevations but to add an additional storey. The then estate surveyor, plainly, did not recommend strongly for consistency as a virtue in itself in this location, notwithstanding the more or less contemporary rejection of a proposal for building in Gascoyne road unless it could be made to a style matching what existed. No doubt it was all a matter of degree[92].

On the other hand there was constant learning from experience. Delays by builders in executing their agreements, such as that of the Innes brothers in completing their Bentham road agreement of 1860, ensured that in the mass development years of 1863 onwards builders were obliged to keep up a steady progress, leases being granted in small batches and some withheld until all were finished.

The lost tribe

Of the builders and developers themselves only the most rudimentary personal detail is now traceable. In several cases a pattern of eastward movement from Islington and the de Beauvoir estate is observable, followed occasionally by a departure for south of the Thames after Hackney projects had flowered. In some cases, already noted, the rise (if the expression is allowable) from journeyman to developer within the area is observable; in other cases, the reverse happened (Thomas Blackmore had to give up his building agreement on the north side of Cassland road, and is later found working as a site foreman on the Crown estate[93]). Even in traceable probate records significant clues as to the personal and professional lives of these men are rare; there is only the bare family data of the census, which occasionally give away that a Butters or a Bagge is a Norfolk man - hence the rationale for the naming of a villa or a terrace emerges. Hardly ever is there sufficient continuity of data to show a curve of growth, if any, in any individual's complement of employees. William Norris has by far the most extensive stable workforce identified, although one suspects that the difference between him and (say) his neighbour Charles Butters may have been more in style than in scale. Probate data is cryptic and ambivalent, family information rare.

Although they are indeed, in Summerson's phrase, a lost tribe, what little is found of South Hackney's identifiable builders and active developers - as opposed to identifiable consumers and house investors - is given in Appendix 2.

Well street and Grove street in 1831

Part Three: Gardens into Suburb

Before Systematic Development

At the realisation of Gigney's assets at the Green Dragon auction, Gigney's interest, and hence not only the ground rents to the land on which Hackney terrace and neighbouring houses had been built, but his undeveloped and unlet land to the east, was acquired by Thomas Whalley. A merchant, based in Friday street near St Paul's, he had originally taken an underlease from Gigney in the neighbourhood of the Three Colts tavern at Grove street, and who, at the time of his own bankruptcy in 1800 (resulting in another auction, this time at Cornhill, under the direction of William Fellowes), had in addition substantial land in Globe town and Bonners Hall, Bethnal Green[94].

By the time the Cass estate was surveyed in 1806, the western part of Gigney's former land had settled into the state it was to assume for the next 40 years - in effect, until the 1785 lease fell in. There were by this time three houses to the west of the terrace, one set well back from the road. In 1800 a chapel had been built at the junction with Well street, founded by George Collison, of the Evangelical Association for the Propagation of the Gospel, otherwise known as the "Village Itineracy"; it was this body that was later to found its theological college in Well street, a little to the west on the site of the present Orchard school[95].

Information about Thomas Whalley's successor, William Carter, remains elusive, as does the origin of further building between 1806 and 1817 along the line of Cassland road, still further east. This took the form of a long terrace known as Hackney Bay, or as on Cross's "New Plan of London" of 1847, Botany Bay. That the area may have been settled by sailors discharged after the Napoleonic war is suggested by the pub, the "Three Mariners", which survived the surrounding shanties, and indeed was eventually rebuilt. Be that as it may, Benjamin Clarke (who went about the area as a general practitioner from the 1840's onwards, and seems, rather to his own surprise, to have been treated as immune from the attentions of the local muggers so far east of the limit of the Hackney terrace street lighting) gives us some idea of the characteristics of this area by telling us it was "bordered on either side by garden plots, and here and there small shanties - the dwellings of the gardeners themselves". John Ridge, the owner of a 13 acre brickfield which now forms part of Victoria Park, was an undertenant in this area, and may well have been associated with its development. After 1845, when the main thrust of development was under way on the Cass estate, this settlement, with the other working-class housing represented by the earlier developments such as those at Nursery place and Baker's row, disappeared into history[96].

Mare street

Whereas in Rocque's time the western cluster of settlement in South Hackney was centred around the Triangle and thence northwards in ribbon fashion along Mare street, by the time of Starling's survey of 1831 it had not only been joined to Shoreditch by ribbon development along (and on either side of) the Hackney road, but had crept eastwards along Well street. The substantial terraces in Mare street and Hackney grove had been added to in Sutton place and architecturally surpassed by the Paragon. Northwards, there had been further terraced housing to rival Hackney terrace at Clapton Common, and villa development there and at Lower Clapton, by the Tyssens; at Stoke Newington, by Thomas Cubitt and Samuel Fox. But Hackney had not yet experienced as intensely the pressure of outward movement from the City that had changed the face of Islington by this time.

In anticipation of the building, towards the end of the second decade of the new century, of the Regent's canal, the South Hackney estate through which it had been cut, previously settled on her marriage on Caroline Bond Hopkins, was sold at auction by her trustees, and ownership so fragmented that North (Northiam) and Vyner streets were filled up by 1831 by small houses with damp cellars, of such a kind that they never attracted inhabitants other than those in the poorest paid occupations. The canal itself and the surroundings of the Triangle became, naturally enough, a focus for the businesses of builders and their suppliers[97].

In Well street, the most notable development was the local resident Hylton Dennis Hacon's Denmark place, 10 terraced houses on the south side, west of Shore place, built on a 46 year lease from St Thomas's hospital. There had also been building, between 1802 and 1821, on building leases from the parish granted to benefit Sir Thomas Vyner's charity. On the north side, a terrace of four late 18th century houses and a pair of adjacent semi's had been built, the former in 1785, possibly for the then occupier, Abraham Jackson; the latter, of earlier date, survive in the form of "Shuttleworth's hotel". St Thomas's place (formerly "Banister Alley", possibly after a member of the Flight family), saw the building between 1805-7 of a terrace of eight, by Thomas Pearson on a 61-year building lease from St Thomas's Hospital. Three other houses built under the same lease at the foot of the pathway on Well street itself were rebuilt well after the main development of the remaining estate[98].

There had been sufficient growth of South Hackney to justify the building, in 1806 by local subscription, of a chapel of ease to the parish church of St John-at-Hackney at the foot of St Thomas's place; this became the parish church on the three-way division of St John at Hackney parish in 1825.

In Tryon's place, nos. 8-10 Tudor road - difficult to date - and a Rectory had been built on the south side. Next to the Rectory, about 1843-4, H.D. Hacon built a further, rather smaller terrace, nos. 14-28 Tudor road, on a former paddock, the backland, taking advantage of the laying out of King Edward's road, becoming the stylistically similar group now numbered 9-15[99]. To the north, the fields between South Hackney and Hackney itself were filling up slowly. St Thomas's granted all but one of the individual leases for the Paragon in 1810 to Robert Collins, carpenter and builder (Sutton place being a contemporary development with which he was connected). Between 1813 and 1820 Chatham place was also developed by the Collins family[100].

Well street

In 1804, the Cass trustees noted that a new road - Grove road - was being made from Mile End which would enhance the value of their estate for building. However, they were at the time in no position to build themselves or even to control building by others. There was practically no systematic building in South Hackney after the Hackney terrace development until the 1840's[101].

The exceptions were in Greenwood's row, now Kingshold road, where during the early years of the century a row of semi-detached villas with gardens had appeared; the patches of development on the St Thomas's estate; and, just outside the parish boundary, the laying out of terraces of small houses on the north side of Well street. These appeared after the war ended, the most southerly, either side of the junction with Elsdale street being known as Waterloo terrace, with Williams terrace south of Collent street and Brunswick terrace south of that, of which remnants (including the "Brunswick Arms") still survive. At the junction with Morning lane the buildings were known as Camomile terrace, and it may have seemed prudent to institute a reminder that this was still essentially a country village.

Indeed the backland was laid out for building by the owner, the auctioneer and professional land speculator William Bradshaw, as early as 1831, and between the late 1830's and about 1843, just beyond the boundaries of the parish, Bradshaw built up a small network of streets to the north of Well street - Margaret, Arthur and Brunswick streets[102].

Grove street

Bradshaw had also acquired a small field in Grove street which fell just outside the area designated for the Park, and by 1845 had let it on building leases to Joseph Sacker, a Rotherhithe publican, whose builder was R. C. Nunn. Thus were formed the 70 or so houses and shops that were Victoria and Albert Groves (capitalising neatly on the royal aura of the Park) and the north side of what became (after one of the Commissioners of Works) Morpeth Road. Here, no doubt with a shrewd eye to the expected demise of the Three Colts, was built a public house, and a protest entered when a substantial source of its business looked likely to be cut off by the stopping up of the old footpath across the fields from Bethnal Green when the Park was formed.

George Wales, the Cass estate surveyor, considered that from the viewpoint of his employer's interests this whole development was "of such a miserable character that it is fortunate that it is so secluded"[103].

Smaller developments included the present 132-8 Lauriston road, dating probably from between 1824 and 1831, behind which the cowkeeper William Eagle had his premises. On the north side of the present line of Wetherell road a row of urban cottages called Providence row, the homes of a population employed in local service trades, was in existence by 1811. The Three Colts was replaced not only by another pub of the same name on the west side of Grove street (subsequently rebuilt as the Empress of India) but by the Swiss Cottage, opposite[104].

The Norris estate had devolved, in 1803, on Henry Handley Norris, then curate at St John at Hackney church, and later the first Rector of South Hackney until his death in 1850. Throughout this time he lived at the house his grandfather had built in Grove street, rather than at the Rectory established in Tryon's place. Prominent in High church affairs and the Church school movement, he was the last of his family to make his home in Hackney, redesigning the park attached to the mansion for the first time since his grandfather's time.

Hackney Wick

On the extreme east, the silk mills of Leny Smith and Co. had gone out of business about 1840, and were in the hands of the Hope Insurance Company until sold by auction to various speculators in the mid 1840's. These speculators included Marmaduke Matthews of Cambridge Heath and Sir John Musgrove. Matthews, and his partner Wilkinson, in so far as brickmaking activities did not temporarily postpone development, built small houses along Wick road (of which those that remain at the north eastern end are not untypical), selling freeholds where they could[105]. The Wick road ribbon development was completed by 1860. Musgrove (also a considerable landowner in Homerton and elsewhere) retained and developed his purchase, Silk Mill row, which had apparently been rebuilt or re-fronted in 1820. He failed to interest the Cass estate in taking this property off his hands. When his residuary estate was sold in 1883 it included 14 cottages on this site, at least 4 of which he built or rebuilt[106]. For a decade beginning about 1852, George Hedger of Bloomsbury (and subsequently of Hyde Park) was to build up similar but new small houses on his field to the north of Cassland road[107].

For the most part these various housing developments were either sold freehold, or leased and then conveyed as freeholds whenever the opportunity arose. Thus there was an obvious tendency, where an estate owner's holding was relatively small and his motive merely short-term profit, for him not to be inclined to create, or at any rate to retain, reversions on leases which would undoubtedly give him management headaches beyond what was justified by the returns involved. North street and Wick road were far from untypical. There is every likelihood that the quality of these developments exerted in none too subtle a way its influence on the marketability of the building land belonging to the larger and inevitably more ambitious estates.

The Parr Estate

Towards the end of the 18th century a small estate in Grove street, south and west of its junction with Well street but north of the Norris estate, had been owned and farmed by John Wowen, who came of a family of sugar refiners long associated with Hackney; and his tenant, Paul de la Pierre, a gentleman of Swiss descent who ran a boys' school in Well street[108]. After Wowen's death the land came into the hands of a Scots family by the name of Currie, subject to the life interest of Wowen's widow, Jane. Jane died in 1838, but the Currie family did not enjoy their property long. The purchaser, Malcolm Currie, had died in 1836, and by 1843 his heir, James Neil Currie, was bankrupt. Once again an estate in South Hackney was divided into plots and put under the auctioneer's hammer[109].

At this time, and indeed until full-scale development took place on the Norris estate, Grove street took a line to the east of the present Lauriston road and Church crescent. From the junction with Grove street lane (the eastern arm of Victoria park road) there ran a footpath, some nine feet across between tall hedges, all the way to the present junction of Lauriston road with Well street. In the 1890's, long after full building up of the area, the local doctor Benjamin Clarke recalled his daily journey as a child from his home in Mare street to Mrs Todd's infant school behind this path[110].

In 1834 Henry Handley Norris gave land to the east of the path for the parish charity school[111]. In the preceding year, Jane Wowen had let a house - probably that Clarke recalls as Mrs Todd's - on the west side of the path to one Thurlby, for conversion into a brewery[112]. The Currie trustees, for all we know continuing a scheme of the bankrupt's own, envisaged building on either side of so much of this path as passed through their land, and intended to improve the road to encourage this to happen. There was as yet no hint of developing the gardens and orchard. Clarke was by this time a young man in his early twenties; when the Currie estate was put up for auction, the rural Hackney he had grown up in was on the point of passing into history.

Plots passed into a variety of hands. The north-easterly corner was bought by Henry Norris V as the site for his father's new church of St John of Jerusalem. William Dupree, already tenant of Thurlby's brewery, bought it outright, and was later to build beside it the Albion pub. From here (so say his advertisements) he would undertake to deliver his XXXX ale to all parts of London. Just to the south, the Hampden (Baptist) chapel was built, for an offshoot of the congregation at St Thomas's Square, on the northern part of land laid out by the vendors as three building plots with a frontage of 150 feet, and sold to Thomas Robinson for £215[113].

Thomas Fullager took on the north east corner of the site, on the corner with

Cassland road; by 1850, this had been developed as a terrace of small houses optimistically called Park terrace. On the island site, just north of the plot destined for the new church, Fullager's builder Samuel Abell put up a similar row, called Park place, on former market garden land[114].

The proprietors of the Hackney Theological Seminary and Society for the Propagation of the Gospel, which had been established in the chapel at the west end of Hackney terrace for upwards of 40 years, establishing their college on Wowen land before 1836, expanded into some existing buildings, on the south side of Well street. The Hackney Theological college, as it came to be known, expanded yet again in 1856 as a result of a purchase from the Parr family, who had set aside land on their building estate "for a religious purpose"[115].

The garden ground and orchard of which the remaining Currie land consisted was taken by John Parr. Parr was a cooper, with a business in Seething lane in the City, and his son, Samuel, was a surveyor and builder (operating from Upper street in Islington). They had an eye to building development[116].

It was Parr who, about 1844, built nos. 50-54 Lauriston road, as St John's terrace, originally a group of four. Like Pickering and his Hackney terrace partners, the style he chose was essentially an urban one, abandoning what would otherwise still have been the country village atmosphere of this corner of the area. One of the houses was for his own occupation, making him, again like Pickering, that rare urban phenomenon a resident developer/landlord.

Apart from his own terrace, Parr was slow to start building operations, but from 1850 onwards development gathered pace. Manor road (Holcroft road) was laid out, the north eastern corner plot going to Alfred Butler, a surgeon, of Well street (this was later known as Hertford House, and still stands), and its neighbour to Thomas Kelsey, resident of Hackney terrace and developer in Cassland road. In December William Thomerson, a builder from the Hackney road, concluded an agreement with Parr for laying out New Church road (Balcorne street), behind what then as now was a narrow entrance onto Well street, and for the demolition and rebuilding of "two ancient messuages" on the site[117].

In the following year Thomerson took 90 year leases of some 40 houses facing each other east and west across the street, of which numbers 25 to 35, complete with pediment, are all that is left to demonstrate the scale and the charm of the street as it must originally have been. These remaining half dozen are typical, with the exception of the eight houses south and west of the eastward swing of the road, which were envisaged as having only three rooms, the stipulated minimum otherwise being five.

Parr was willing to part with his land either leasehold or freehold. At the time, the market in the area was in the developer's favour rather than the landlord's, hence the term of 90 years acquired by Thomerson: in mid-century, a 90 year term almost invariably denoted houses at the smaller end of the range. Among the purchasers of a freehold for building were a group of jewellers, mainly from Clerkenwell, representing the Goldsmiths and Jewellers Annuity Institution, who in May 1851 took a plot some 180 feet by 50 - neither very wide nor very deep - in Manor road (Holcroft road) for the building of almshouses. When built, to a Gothic design by W. P. Griffiths not unsympathetic to the earlier rebuilding of Monger's, these provided accommodation for six households[118].

Other freehold plots went to William Davis, a baker of Old Ford, who employed William Norris to design and build for him a large mansion at the rear and nine terraced houses in the front of the plot immediately west of what became the site of the Clarendon Arms; and to the Theological college. John Mate, police sergeant in Well street, paid £70 in 1852 for the plot on the north side of Balcorne street on which he had built the cottages nos. 47 and 49 (the speculator behind the other half of this small terrace is, if different, not known)[119].

John Parr senior died in April 1853, and the estate was inherited by Samuel, who took over the house in St John's terrace. It was he who in September 1854 concluded a deal with Thomas Heath, beer seller from Newington Green, for a 40 year lease of

Manor Villas.

Villas, now demolished, on the east side of Manor (Holcroft) road

"the free public house called or intended to be called the Clarendon Arms". The lease does not record who put up this elegant building, but it was more than likely William Turner[120]. Turner, like Thomerson, had come north and east from a previous scene of building operations on the Bethnal Green side of Hackney road, and seems to have been a participant in most of the remaining building in New church road, financed by Samuel Parr on mortgage, and in Manor road. The exception was the site of the four most southerly houses on the west side. These seem to have been built under an agreement concluded with John Hunn, a local carpenter, who got into difficulties; after he had taken a lease of the first two, the next pair were taken over by and conveyed to Turner, together with the remainder of the west side of Manor road south of the Goldsmiths' and Jewellers' Almshouses, for the sum of £490 for a term of 88 years. Turner himself lived in the largest in the terrace, no. 19, which he called Clarendon Cottage, for nearly 20 years, moving thereafter to the grander Cedars, in Banbury road[121].

Some time after 1857 Samuel Parr left South Hackney for Oak Hall, East Ham, and his brother John moved into St John's terrace. After this time the family seem to have lost interest in the reversion of the remaining freehold estate, as Samuel seems to have been involved in the building of Manor terrace on the east side of Manor road, but parted with his interest in this and other neighbouring land. John Parr junior, who had taken over the cooperage business in Seething lane, may have bought him out of the St John's terrace property, as in 1863 he is found raising a £500 mortgage on his residence and the Hunn lease[122].

It is likely that neither generation of Parrs ever intended a long term future for their association with the estate; perhaps the question was never considered. Certainly its very size must have contributed to this. The terms of the leases they granted were not synchronised, with 70, 90 and 88 year terms being granted to fall in at a variety of different dates; and the substantial proportion of their acreage disposed of as freeholds put continued control of the estate as a whole out of the question. The building of 96-102 Balcorne street in part of the back gardens of St John's terrace is an early example of infilling.

Alfred Chinn must have been grateful to be free of the constraints of a strict landlord. A successful manufacturer, with a long-standing business in Harman street, Kingsland road, he arranged, at some time around 1890, for a large stucco panel to be created on the flank wall of his home at no. 4 St John's terrace (50 Lauriston road), and for there to be inscribed in it the following advertisement, still just visible:

ALFRED CHINN
MANUFACTURER OF BOXES
FOR JEWELLERS, CHEMISTS,
PERFUMERS, ETC.

As will be seen in a later chapter, this would scarcely have been acceptable on the Cass estate.

The Cass Estate

Planning for development

By the earliest years of the 19th century the Cass trustees had identified the interest of the estate in ensuring good quality building development. In 1824, they refused to bind themselves to grant leases to prospective builders on the Gigney land on the expiry of the 1785 lease. Well aware of the inferiority of much of the existing development, particularly on Gigney and Greenwollers leasehold property, by mid-decade they began to plan actively for taking possession at the end of 1846 of the bulk of their estate. In October 1845 a special Hackney estates committee was formed, and systematically made site inspections[123].

On the one hand, the Park had been established, although the intended high quality Crown estate villas had yet to materialise; there were regular and frequent horse bus services to the City and the West End. On the other, as has been noted, the estate was fringed by development of a character that caused some dismay to the estate surveyor, the energetic 27 year old George Wales, appointed in September 1845.

Wales was required to live on the estate, and to provide regular attendance at an office there, for the purpose of receiving rents and general superintendence of disbursements. He established a drawing office, and here the formation of new roads and sewers were planned, as well as building agreements drawn up and plans and elevations of houses revised and discussed. For these purposes the old Jackson house at the west end of Hackney terrace was rebuilt, Wales paying £75 annually for a 14 year lease of it; there was consequent alteration to the front entrance to no. 1 Hackney terrace. An estate office was added at the side. Attendance would be provided during ordinary office hours by Wales himself, or one of his clerks if his continuing surveyor's practice in the City required his presence elsewhere.

Wales had enormous difficulty in discovering, 61 years after the grant of Gigney's lease, to whom it was he should present bills for dilapidations of leased property, such was the complexity of underletting and assignment of leases that had taken place during the currency of the lease. The first lesson absorbed by the trustees from the Gigney experience was that in future they would never grant a lease which permitted the lessee to underlet without their express consent.

No effort was spared to "raise the tone" of the estate, as Wales put it. Numerous properties were found to have come to the end of their useful life; Fletcher's gardens and Hackney Bay were cleared, and the writing was on the wall for Nursery place. A long hard look at Hackney terrace itself was necessary. Lamp irons were removed as obsolete. The walls round the Lawn, the private garden on the present site of Meynell crescent, had fallen into disrepair, and some solution, not too expensive, and preferably not involving draining the moat at its boundary, had to be found. A policy towards lettings was adopted; requests for long leases were refused, and the houses, as they fell vacant, were relet on annual tenancies at a rent of £30. Increasingly, as large villas were built elsewhere (in King Edward's road, on the St Thomas's estate in particular), Hackney terrace became relatively harder to let, old tenants removing themselves to the fashionable and spacious new premises, and new tenants insisting on the provision of water closets as a condition of taking a house.

The trustees had to address their minds to management of the Hackney terrace lawn, as the arrangements under the 1796 leases whereby this had been democratically managed by the tenants themselves had, at the end of the term, automatically come to an end. A plan to permit its use by the boys resident in the school at neighbouring Common house was vigorously opposed by tenants, and came to nothing, indeed their later use of the field to the east gave rise to complaint. Not anxious to lose control, the trustees drew up a set of rules themselves, and envisaged that the surveyor, himself a near neighbour, would manage the lawn and enforce the rules.

New planting of young trees took place. No use of the lawn other than "for the purposes of a pleasure ground" would be countenanced; cricket, and "any other game that injures the grass plot" were expressly prohibited. No-one was to use the lawn as a drying-ground, or for beating carpets or furniture. Servants were excluded unless they "had the care of a child or children"; so, for that matter, were dogs. Smoking was forbidden, except between 9 at night and 9 in the morning; and any infringement of the rules or damage to the plants or shrubs might lead not only to the bill for replacements being presented to the tenant whose child or servant was responsible, but to the blocking up of the access gate in the offender's garden wall. Tenants were enjoined not to leave the gate to the Common open, in case horses and cattle grazing there might stray in; and the gate was in any event secured at night. These threats were not idle, one tenant whose children were persistently an irritation to neighbours being given notice to quit[124].

Monger's almshouses

One of the messiest problems that had to be resolved in the mid-1840's review arose in relation to Monger's almshouses, which lay to the south and west of Common house, the house built by Thomas Riddle on an underlease from Gigney, and subsequently used as a boys' boarding school.

The almshouses had been built in 1669, endowed by a bequest from Henry Monger, who left the land and £400 to create a residence for six "poor, civil, honest" men of the parish of Hackney who had reached 60 years or thereabouts. He directed that the building be in brick, and "in such manner and form as near as can be to the Clothworker's almshouses in the parish of Islington"[125]. It does not seem that this was followed exactly, as the almshouses in Frog lane, Essex Road were a good deal plainer than the pretty building with its central Dutch gable that the benefactor's trustees produced.

Some ten years after Monger's death, the annuity of £12 he had left for repairs to the property and fuel for the residents was augmented by a further bequest. In 1679, Joanna Martin (who as executor, with Thomas Cass, was associated with the early administration of the trust) left to the parish the plot of land immediately to the west of the almshouses, on which stood two weatherboarded houses, which were subsequently taken down and replaced by what were later described as "two tolerable houses and five smaller ones". These were thenceforth known as the "endowment houses", the income they produced enhancing the ability of the Monger trustees to maintain their six poor, civil and honest charges[126].

Until 1800, the affairs of the Monger charity appear to have been administered first by the Cass family and, after the death of Sir John's widow Elizabeth, by the Cass trustees: indeed the building was known on occasion as the Cass almshouses. When however in that year the Rector, Archdeacon Watson, made enquiries, the trustees could not give a satisfactory account of their acquisition of the power they were asserting to appoint new beneficiaries for the charity. Nor was this all: the practice they employed, of permitting the men to have their wives live with them, and to stay on as widows after a husband's death - contrary to the exact terms of the bequest - was alleged to derive only from the policy, humane though it was, of Dame Elizabeth Cass. The Rector had the practice stopped; the parish asserted, successfully, its own right to run the charity's affairs[127].

Common management had tended towards indiscriminate letting, which itself created difficulty for both Cass's and Monger's charities, compounded by individuals such as James Reeve being tenant of adjacent property of both. By the late 1840's the exact boundary between the endowment land and Cass's property had become obscured by common occupation.

George Wales and the Cass trustees had, moreover, quite radical plans. They saw Hackney terrace, and the building land opposite, as one of the centrepieces of their developed estate, and wanted it to be approached by a commensurately grand and open roadway, to be called Terrace road, improving at the same time the approaches to Terrace lodge and Common house. The natural line for such a road, they thought, was through the site of the almshouses and the adjacent endowment houses. These were in poor condition; so much was common ground between the Cass trustees and the parish authorities, acting as the Monger trustees. So the Cass trustees came forward in March 1846 with an offer. They would build 4 houses, valued at £18 annual rental each, as endowment; and provide a freehold site for new almshouses, plus a "building bonus" of £100. It was a tempting offer[128].

It fell through on the question of the site. The parish authorities took advice from E.C. Hakewill, then engaged on building the new church of St John of Jerusalem, who farmed out the problem to an assistant, William Grellier. Grellier was not impressed. The offer was a freehold conveyance of the triangle of land now bounded by Terrace road, yet to be built, on the east, Grove street on the west, and Cassland road on the north.

This was, said Grellier, too surrounded by roads and (in those days before metalling) too prone to dust. If the houses were built to a uniform pattern, as they must be "to preserve the almspeople from jealousy", there would not be enough room for ornamental garden ground. More than that: the site was overlooked by houses which were "generally of an inferior character" (this can only have been a reference to Park terrace, the houses recently built on Currie land, on the west side of Lauriston road; or to the old Gigney houses on the north east corner of the junction of Cassland road and Well street). As it was, the almshouses had in their existing situation the benefit of the southern prospect to the new Church (completed in 1847/8) and Norris's park, and to the north "gentlemen's pleasure grounds" - the rear garden of the school, and Hackney terrace lawn.

Grellier estimated new almshouses would cost about £700 to build: this proved to be a considerable underestimate. He went on to match it with a corresponding overestimate. If the new site was not accepted, he considered, the endowment houses could be rebuilt at about £1400 for 3 houses, and could certainly be let at about £50 per annum, which he considered "very moderate, looking at rents of £60-65 in Islington, Peckham, Brompton and Dalston".

The site was probably not large enough for each of five houses to be built on a scale to command such a rent, looking at Wales's £75 for his own residence. Equally if not more seriously, Grellier was in complete ignorance of where the rear boundaries of the property actually lay, and once the trustees had rejected the Cass offer on the basis of his advice, they found that they had much less room for manoeuvre than everyone had been assuming. In September, it was established that the boundary was in fact none other than the back wall of the endowment houses. Here was a crisis: when Reeve's lease fell in, at the end of the year, the endowment houses would be deprived of their "outbuilding conveniences". Rebuilding was urgent.

In this both sides were agreed. Indeed, Wales took the view (his roles as Cass surveyor and neighbour coinciding) that "the present tenantry are such as I should regret to see prolonged"[129]. He stepped in, and negotiated an arrangement with the Cass trustees whereby there was an exchange of land, Monger's giving up a little at the western end of the endowment houses for the formation of Terrace road, and gaining a little of what they had previously believed was theirs, at the backs of the houses. He also negotiated an arrangement with John Clark, a City solicitor, whereby Clark offered to finance the rebuilding of all but the central, relatively recently built pair of the houses then on the site, this remaining pair to be re-roofed and have new entrance porches. He would put up "three neat houses, at £24 p.a. each", and a pair of semi's at £27 alongside the pair that were to remain. For this outlay of £2100 he asked for a 60 year lease, and offered a ground rent of £60, which he considered "too high for any speculator"; certainly it compared well from the charity's point of view with ground rents on offer in Victoria Park road, say, within the next ten years[130].

Clark was not truly a speculator. He was the Registrar to the Cass charity trustees; more than that, he was a neighbour, being the tenant of Grove Cottage, north west of Hackney terrace on the other side of the road. The interests of his charity and the amenity of his local environment motivated his taking a financial interest in Monger's problems.

There is little doubt, moreover, but that the new houses, built in 1847-8 (the entire row being known thereafter as 1-7 Blenheim cottages, now Church crescent) were designed by Wales, the new pair of semi's, at the eastern end of the plot, being of a similar size and shape to the retained and improved pair, if not otherwise to match. In the terrace of three at the western end he let himself go rather more, with a little unpretentious Gothic. The gardens were extended northwards in 1858 under a lease to John Clark's widow, a matter which was to give the trustees and Wales some trouble shortly afterwards.

In his next venture, the rebuilding of the almshouses themselves, Wales went Tudor. In May 1848 he had come forward with another offer to the Monger trustees. He proffered a plan for new almshouses, which would cost some £1100 to build; realising that the charity could only afford £750 of this, he offered to bear the difference, if it were to be treated as an outstanding debt repayable over 15 years, with interest, out of the rents of Blenheim cottages. His professional services he offered free, "my feelings being excited", he later wrote, "to try and aid my friend Mr Clark's houses"[131].

The plans were approved in June 1848, and the building completed the following January. Sadly, the arrangement went sour, which can only because Wales failed to make clear to his clients what his offer did not include. He found that in addition to receiving the assistance they had already had from him, the trustees expected him to pay the £20 cost of airing the building and planting and turfing the garden. His protests only elicited £10 in two annual instalments - the charity had no other income than that from its founder and from the endowment houses - so he declined to intervene when there were complaints about the windows being defective. The dispute had not been resolved by 1851, so the trustees refinanced their debt, and the parties parted company[132].

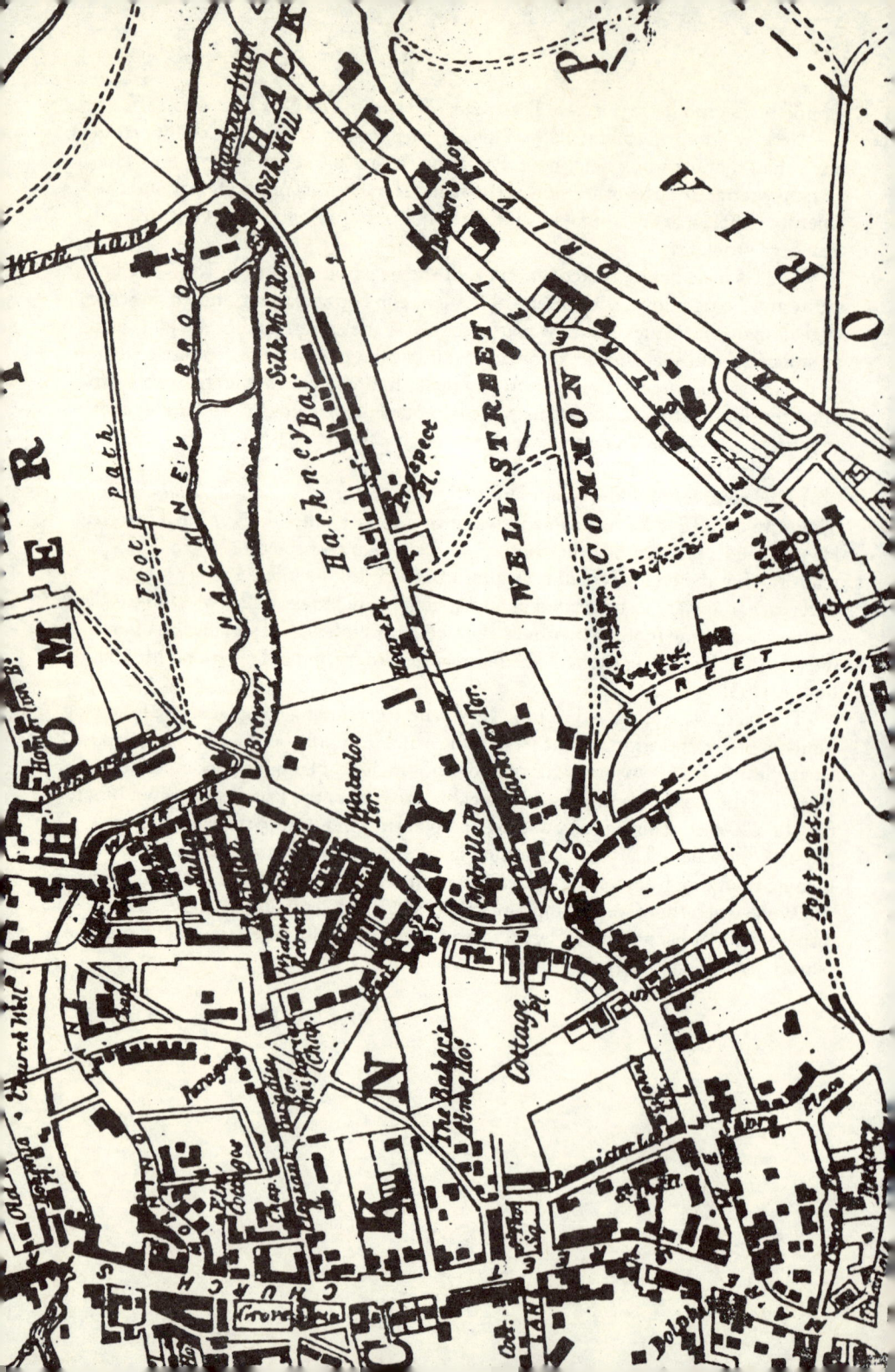

"To be let on building lease...."

Originally the Cass estate was very enclosed. Road layout on the northern part of the estate proved straightforward enough, and roads on this part began to be formed as early as 1846[133]. The estate's western boundary was however a field's breadth away from Cambridge Heath road, and direct access would only possible from Well street or Grove street: King Edward's road, even had it been opened up earlier than it was, could scarcely have been called direct.

Access from the main London to Hackney road was essential for a prime development, and the key was the market garden, formerly of Mary Wells but by the late 1840's in the hands of William Rea, fronting onto Cambridge Heath road by a row of houses, of the 1820's, called Cambridge terrace. Negotiations starting in 1847, building land and a narrow aperture onto the main road were acquired, Rea also disposing of part at least of Cambridge terrace to the builder William Norris[134].

This narrow aperture proved the key to development not only of the likeliest area of the Cass estate, but also the alignment with St Thomas's land and unlocking the enclosed Hickling orchard. Shore road and St Thomas's road could be so laid out as to afford a satisfactory grid pattern; and the Crown estate integrated, land exchanges ensuring that the northern boundary of the Victoria Park building land was the new Victoria Park road. Only Henry Norris V, now managing his father's estate, resisted, for a time, Wales's badgering for a land exchange, but by 1850 this was in hand, and the plans crystallised as a published layout, called grandly "the North Eastern Portion of the Metropolis, prepared to shew the contemplated Improvements in the Cassland Estate, Victoria Park etc." Roads in the northern part had been given names commemorating past Cass treasurers, and the monarch regnant in the year of the charity's foundation. The name "Cassland" was a brainwave of Wales's own[135].

Although it was never expressly stated, a different perception of the north eastern and south western parts of the estate is apparent. The class of housing for which offers for building agreements were accepted was larger, more spacious and usually in larger parcels in the south and west, whereas small builders were permitted to take plots for one or two houses of smaller size in the north east. Here, also, in 1848, probably as a result of Wales responding to a press advertisement in May of that year, George Oldfield, of Chard in Somerset, established a ropeworks north of what was to become Bentham road, and bounding the ribbon development along Wick road. There is no sign of this on the 1850 plan, and indeed the arrangement may not have been formalised until 1851, when a lease was granted, and Oldfield began the first building on the southern frontages of his holding[136]; but also, no doubt, it was not a feature that the marketing scheme wished to emphasise.

The first building agreement the estate secured, in 1848, was for a large detached house in Gascoyne road. Complete with coach-house and stable, this imposing residence was let on an 80 year lease to an affluent gentleman who moved there from

Detail from Turner's 1847 map of Hackney

Wellington terrace, St John's Wood. This was George Wales's own father[137].

Other building agreements, for a further villa and for semi's, followed, and with this success, however stage-managed, to his credit, Wales junior could market the estate more effectively. A lithograph* was commissioned, showing mirror-images of the Wales villa, flanking semi-detached houses in the same style, suitably enhanced in the manner of artists' impressions, and was published by Waterlows:

To be let on building leases. Plots of land for villas on the same line of frontage as the Buildings shown on this lithograph. The situation is remarkably pleasant, having a due south aspect and overlooking Well Street Common and Victoria Park. The distance from the Royal Exchange is less than 3 miles. Apply to Mr Wales, Cassland Estate office, Hackney." [138]

Results were poor, not to say disastrous. By 1860, no further building had taken place in Gascoyne road.

No more was advertising more generally for builders producing the kind of response Wales or the trustees had in mind, despite attempts to demonstrate the proximity of the Cass estate to the Park. And, as has been noted, Wales badgered the Crown authorities to make progress with their own plans. The trustees laid this early failure at the door of the legal restrictions - to be eased in 1853 - on the development of charity land, and the remoteness and enclosed nature of the estate.

In June 1851 however, they entered into two building agreements, for widely differing kinds of house at opposite ends of the estate. It is evident that three main focal points for development had been identified. One was the old focus of Well street, pushed eastwards towards Kenton road and the new ropeworks; the second focus, along the line of Cassland road; the third was near the settlement round Tryon's place and Mare street, pushed eastwards towards the new park, along Victoria Park road.

Victoria Park road

As a general rule, speculators fixing on the Cass estate at this period confined themselves to two or three properties at a time. There were two exceptions, one on the southern and one on the northern part of the estate. In 1852, J. A. Hughes, formerly of Enfield road, de Beauvoir town, building at the extreme western end of the new road, began implementing an agreement under which he aimed to produce some 24 terraced houses on each side, in groups of varying lengths, the southern line ending in a pub. The style varied, but was in general plain, with the barest window ornamentation. As an experienced builder acting as his own developer raising money on a private mortgage, he had brought his own ideas as to design eastwards, and the influence of the estate surveyor as architect seems to have been limited. After a swift start with his first terrace and the pub, the "Sir John Cass", opposite what later became the end of Fremont street, an early call on the estate was made to grant the resultant leases. Hughes however got into difficulties, his mortgagees eventually being put under formal notice to complete the remainder of his agreement. His only

*cover illustration

surviving building in South Hackney is the contemporary 1-5 Cassland road, the smallest and simplest of all his works[139].

In contrast are the villas on the north side of Victoria park road, between Clermont and Skipworth roads. The first of these to be completed were the pairs of semi's at nos. 113-119, let in 1852 to J. R. Wildman, described as "gentleman, of Alfred street, Bow road", on a lease of 80 years at £13. 2s 6d. each pair. In the following two years the remainder of this stretch was virtually completed with the addition of nos 85-7 (Lexden villas, financed by W. J. Wilson) and nos. 97-99 (Woburn villas, financed by John Waterloo Todd and rented at £17.1s the pair), together with 101-111 (Devonshire terrace, attributable to John Bower, an "eating house keeper" of Shoreditch). The remaining terrace, the surveyor/developer Hugh Eastman's Somerset villas (89-95) of 1860-2 has been most neatly interpolated, matching up almost imperceptibly with the remainder of the block and with nos 81-3, financed and leased in 1855 by a Bethnal Green timber merchant, William Avenell[140].

The architect of any of the pre-Eastman houses cannot be known with certainty, nor can the builder, as all were leased directly, for the estate's preferred 80-year term, to the financiers - who were, in all cases, non-building professionals. The uniformity, and the dignity, of height and arrangement taken together with harmonious variety in detail makes this the most elegant surviving Victorian streetscape in South Hackney. Here must be the influence of Wales's Cassland road estate drawing office.

With one addition, these houses completed the development for private residences of Victoria Park road in the 1850's; the only other building to take place before 1860 was the Norris almshouses, as the Crown estate, owning most of the southern stretch between Redruth road and Hughes's Sir John Cass pub, did not start building until 1860.

The addition was Fern villas, a pair of semi's erected on the south side of the road, immediately to the east of the (later) Royal Standard pub. This development was one of that select class which were financed by a individuals who provided their own architectural expertise. The developers were a father-and-son partnership, James Lovegrove senior and junior, the latter being Hackney's first ever District Surveyor. His presumed architectural expertise did not prevent Wales returning the original designs as "very indifferent"; and perhaps his prognostication that the partnership was likely to get into difficulties may have been accurate, as this was their only building venture, in South Hackney at any rate[141].

The northern estate

The second of the significant Cass building agreements of 1851 was with John Page, a builder who had been active in the Barnsbury Park area, but who, like many another when he started building, moved into the area of his operations, establishing himself at an address in Terrace road. He insisted on 99 year leases, and developed, as

"Page's cottages", what came ultimately to be known as Elsdale street, but was originally known as West street, and later as Terrace Road West. He leased his houses in groups of four, paying £2.10s. (£2.50) ground rent for each house. The houses themselves were truly cottages, and in scale with the Gigney development around Well street. Unlike the larger villas being built in the neighbourhood whose facilities were internal, they had, as built, water closets accessible from the back yard[142].

Page's cottages, if the most minor beginnings, confirm that the northern aspect of this second phase of Cass developments, whatever the scale on which developers operated, was for smaller dwellings, and less easily let by the landowner, than building at the grander end of the estate in Victoria park road.

In the immediate neighbourhood of Hackney terrace Thomas Kelsey, a textile merchant and resident of the terrace, financed the building, in 1852, of the western end of the row now numbered 4-16 Cassland road, George Jackson being responsible for the remainder. The uniformity of this terrace, despite its different financing, must again indicate the guiding hand of the estate surveyor, in the same way as the uniformity of elevation apparent in the grander terraces built in Victoria park road[143].

From these beginnings, development crept eastwards from the ancient focus of Well street, towards Oldfield's ropeworks in Bentham road, Oldfield himself among others developing small terraced houses on the north side of this road from 1854. (He, or his son, who followed him into the business, is probably also responsible for two surviving villas of the 1860's in Kenton road, nos. 21-3, named after the other focus of his ropemaking business, in Chard.) The pace of development is however summed up in the parish's refusal, for several years in the 1850's, to adopt Kenton road as "not of sufficient utility" to the public.

In the southern part of the new Terrace road, William Cook ran into financial trouble on his small triangular plot at the junction where the road meets Lauriston road (Grove street). The nature of this development, long since demolished, was not much to the liking of John Clark, solicitor and Registrar to the Cass trustees, the developer responsible for Blenheim cottages. His dislike in any of those capacities must have been exacerbated by the fact that he and his wife Martha lived in Grove cottage, the house built in Gigney's day which stood until the end of the century on the site north west of Hackney terrace, and later numbered 7 Cassland road.

As ever, Clark was constructive in his dislike. His first proposal, in October 1852, involved two houses (nos. 42-44) on the southern corner of Terrace road, opposite his own house. He promised the trustees that what would be erected would be "better than builders or speculators would be likely to set up". The neighbouring pair (nos. 38-40) followed, and each was readily leased, at Clark's direction, to gentlemen from the City and from Peckham Rye. Considering that this was not the prime part of the estate and the houses were smaller than the largest in Victoria Park road, the ground rent of £5 would have compared tolerably well from the estate's point of view with what was currently obtainable elsewhere had it been charged on all the houses; in fact the second pair seem to have been granted at a peppercorn[145].

The first pair were completed by June 1853. The following spring, Clark undertook to build a further pair of houses, to a very similar design and specification to the first built, prominent corner houses, at the beginning of the crescent laid out opposite Hackney terrace. The rents he proposed, £5 and £4 respectively, were regarded as on the low side for such a prominent site, but treated as acceptable on the registrar's assurance that there was an offer from "a person of respectability" to lease them if built. The agreement also permitted Clark two years free of rent so far as the second house was concerned, "in consequence of the high price of materials". Wales no doubt provided the design. He and Clark were after Clark's death to incur public criticism for dealing in this manner with their employers at all, let alone the favourable terms secured[146].

In so far as the Registrar intended to encourage others of like mind to invest in his neighbourhood, he had a modest success, as Thomas Gillespy, a City broker resident in Well street followed his example, and took in 1854 the plots for 13-21 Cassland road, to form the first half of the crescent. It is probable that his builder was George Day, who had recently been active in putting up houses (now demolished) on the north side of Bentham road, and who in the same year capitalised on the presence of the ropeworks at the foot of Kenton road by taking the corner plot there, building the Kenton Arms and houses immediately to the east and south of it. If so, Day's reward for the Gillespy enterprise was the lease of no. 23; nos. 13 and 15 (endowments for the two Gillespy daughters) were completed in 1855, and 17 and 19 the following year (these being, with 21, built under a separate agreement taken in June 1856). In 1858 the Cass estate considered the layout of the crescent sufficiently complete to approach tenants for a contribution towards its enclosure, and to invite tenders for railings.

This constituted the end for the time being of the trustees' prime northern development. There were no offers, or at any rate no suitable offers, for the remainder of the building ground in the crescent for the best part of the subsequent decade.

Terrace road was however advancing northwards; Gillespy himself was responsible at least for no. 21, which had formed part of the same plot as 17 in the crescent and which he was, in 1857, granted permission to develop. John Page was also active on the now-demolished west side. The building agreement for 15-19 (15 and 17 being known initially as York villas) seems to have been let in 1858, with completion, and immediate letting on the market, the following year[147].

Completing the St Thomas's estate

The Flight leases falling in in 1848, St Thomas's Hospital prepared a terrier of its South Hackney holdings in that year, and employed Henry Currey to survey the ground. The precise eastward line of King Edward's Road, named for the Hospital's royal benefactor, was projected in that year, although its western limb, linking the Triangle and the ancient focus of the estate at Shore House, had been established since 1842. In that year the Hospital had bought the land necessary for this part of the road from Zillah Hickling, incidentally affording landowners such as Hacon an additional building frontage on the northern side[148].

Further planning to best advantage depended on the co-operation of the estate owners to south and east. Between 1848 and 1850 agreement was evidently reached not only with the Norris family, for the exact line of King Edward's road, but also with the Cass trustees. These latter had some difficulty achieving the most favourable line for their own major artery, although ultimately the alignment of Shore road and St Thomas's (Ainsworth) roads, linking Well street and Victoria park road through both estates, were settled, and in 1850 all three estates published their planned layouts for development[149].

The Cass trustees, as has been discussed in the previous section, were if necessary prepared to let plots in penny numbers, apparently reacting to the initiative of developers. St Thomas's, on the advice of Henry Currey, carved up their estate south of Well street into a number of large building plots. Other than for small-scale infilling on redevelopment of the 18th century sites, the Hospital entered into no agreement for a plot smaller than for nine double-fronted villas. The earliest agreement, in March 1848, on the north west corner of the estate (and therefore unaffected by relationships with neighbouring landowners), was with Charles Butters, a self-made builder from Norfolk[150].

Butters had followed the characteristic pattern of London builders of moderate size in that he had risen from being a journeyman carpenter to master builder, no doubt by the process of himself speculating in sub-contracts. He undertook to build, on the south western corner of the estate south of Tudor road and west of Shore road, houses in a variety of arrangements of terraces and semi's, some 29 in all, for which when sufficiently complete he was granted a 75 year lease at a rent of £99. The first four houses were taken in 1849 by Christopher Framingham, a local investor in house property and his brother Charles; the grandest of all, no. 41, later the builder's own residence, was built for Thomas Kelsey, like an earlier St Thomas's developer a trimmings manufacturer and housing speculator, who was only one of several Hackney terrace residents to move to King Edward's road for its modern space and comfort. Other lessee-investors included Butters's sub-contractor William Rayner (himself more than mid-way through the familiar career pattern of journeyman to building contractor).

Butters went on to conclude other agreements with St Thomas's in 1850 and 1853, and eventually became responsible for most of the south-western part of the building of the St Thomas's Well street estate along King Edward's road, together with houses in Well street on the north east corner of Shore road. One of these,"Norfolk house", later successively a girls' hostel and the Norfolk Hotel for Working Men, became his family home, although he died in 1889 at one of South Hackney's grandest houses, Parkfield villa, which he had originally built on the north side of King Edward's road for Thomas Kelsey.

In 1851, Butters was followed on to the estate by William Norris, one of Hackney's most substantial building contractors (at times he laid claim to the title of surveyor) and prominent citizens, although no relation of the landowning Norrises. He took land on the west side of Shore road, on the south side of Well street, and so much of the estate as lay east of St Thomas's road. Between Butters and Norris, the western portion of the estate, in Tudor road, King Edward's road, Shore road and Well street, was built up gradually throughout the 1850's. Butters on the one hand seemed to turn over much of his land within a couple of years, and was first in the field, so it is not clear why Norris was slow to implement his agreement of 1851, unless he had taken it with the deliberate intention of holding it in reserve pending his pursuance of other projects elsewhere. It may have been this intention that made him hold out, successfully, for 80 year leases as against Butters's 75[151].

His delay was not entirely due to the doldrums of the market in the mid-1850's: his first two leases were taken in 1854, and followed by others in 1856. By this time he was using premises in what is now Tudor grove as machine workshops; once this part of the business was up and running in 1856 the rate of completions advanced noticeably. In 1859, William Norris took a building agreement for the whole of the estate eastwards of St Thomas's road for 80 years, the following decade seeing all of the north side of King Edward's road developed, together with the St Thomas's frontages on Handley and Speldhurst roads which were the product of realignment of the estate's boundaries with Henry Norris.

The only point at which the St Thomas's governors seem to have allowed the kind of ad hoc letting of small plots that was characteristic of the Cass estate was in the old, northern section of Shore road itself, and the neighbouring Well street frontage; but here the main constraint was the existence of building in Shore road and Well street, dating from the Flight lease, which was far from the end of its natural life, leaving scope only for infilling. A charity estate was bound to perceive itself as inhibited from demolition and rebuilding of anything that might produce a profitable rack rent. Hence the late redevelopment of this earliest-developed, prime frontage.

It is difficult to establish how many sub-contractors Butters and Norris relied on; though neither took a substantial proportion of their leases in hand, their building found a ready market amongst investors. Among the identifiable sub-contractors, apart from Rayner who graduated during the course of the estate's completion from working for Butters to working on his own behalf, Norris used Thomas Blackmore and James Kimber, both of whom used their leases as security from Norris's own favoured lender, J.C. Luxmoore of Bayswater[152].

Visually the diversity of the St Thomas's estate, given the sizeable plots taken by the various contractors, suggests strongly that Henry Currey was not required to or did not seek to exercise a guiding hand to secure uniformity or consistency in elevations. There seems to have been only a limited attempt at uniformity in King Edward's road, which ranged from a plain understated Italianate style to curious Dutch gables. Whereas in Victoria Park road and the northern edge of the Cass estate George Wales was imposing such uniformity of approach as was within his power and preference, in the Shore road infilling there was none. No. 26, built in 1855 by Butters (complete with garden grotto) and let to his close business associate, the silk merchant Thomas Peet Glaskin (of whom more later) in January 1856, derives clearly from regency Georgian, although massive by comparison with the then surviving 18th century building in the road, of which no. 18, now the only survivor, was much the largest. Oak Villas (nos. 21-29, opposite), recently demolished in favour of a car park, were built by William Norris in 1857/8 in the same tradition as 26, if plainer and more perfunctorily designed. "Gloucester cottage", however (no.35), another recent victim of the industrialisation of this street, built for J. H. Cuzner, was heavily Italianate, and would have contributed its charm more effectively to the streetscape had it not been completely dwarfed by its neighbours, "Denmark villas" (nos. 37-39) and "Leven villas"[153].

Leven villas, nos. 31-3, of 1856, another William Norris property, are much more in the style of much of King Edward's road. The singularity of Denmark villas, built not by Norris but by J. W. Beetles, must on the other hand be due as much to the lapse of time between its building and that of the remainder of the street. (The naming of this block may have been as much associated with Denmark place, Hacon's Well street development of 1810, as to the heir to the throne's recent Danish marriage.) The Well street frontage, nos. 44-6, adjoining Hacon's development, was developed at the same time as Shore road[154].

Much of the present architectural character of what is now left of Shore road is owed to T. P. Glaskin's infill development of the substantial garden included in his lease of no.26. The grotto flourished only briefly: Glaskin overbuilt to the north at an early date, and developed "Castle villas", nos. 20-22, in partnership with Butters in 1865. This group is all that remains of Butters's contribution to South Hackney architecture.

At the western end of King Edward's road many of the houses were built as large double-fronted semi's, as projected on Henry Currey's 1850 layout, others as short terraces, nonetheless substantial. As the published Currey layout post-dates the earliest building agreement by at least 2 years, it is difficult to regard its indication of the projected density as more than notional, although it is consistent with the earlier, Butters buildings. No doubt the estate would have preferred the eastern estate as built up by Norris in the 1860's to match the western end of their prestige road, but by the 1860's there was less demand for capacious double-fronted housing in South Hackney, and the housing built on the eastern stretches was smaller in scale than what remains on the adjacent streets on Henry Norris's land.

It has been noted that William Norris, having taken the site for Oak and Leven villas on the north west corner of the junction of Shore and Tudor roads, did not complete either until after 1856. In the meantime he was completing the development of this corner site, taking nos. 53-55 in 1854 and 1856, and nos. 61-63 in 1857 (the latter bearing the same classical keystone motifs above the front door as characterise his Percy villas, nos. 66-8 Well street, of the same year). Indeed the antiquarian enthusiasm for the name "Percy" in this area, commemorating the family's medieval association with Brooke House - the allusion now represented chiefly by the Northumberland Arms - seems to have William Norris as its common factor. He renamed Greenwood's row as Percy road, and himself moved into 72 Well street, part of the terrace he called Percy villas, around 1859. (Nos. 39-43 Well street, at the foot of St Thomas's place, are sometimes found to be referred to as Percy terrace; the site of these appears to have formed part of the plot developed by Thomas Pearson following his building agreement of 1805; although evidently rebuilt in the mid-19th century, with these, as with Northumberland houses, there is no obvious link with Norris.)

A further Hospital agreement in 1851 for the west side of St Thomas's road was with John Pearson, then resident in Shore road and seemingly an investor on the Glaskin model rather than a building professional such as Butters or Norris. Here development was just as slow as on Norris's land, the first completion being nos. 26-34, financed by Thomas Gillespy and completed in October 1857. Speed of development can have gained nothing from the death, in 1854, of Pearson himself, and the remainder of his agreement was completed for his executors between 1862 and 1867 by William Turner, giving rise to the two substantial terraces at nos. 6-20 St Thomas's (Ainsworth) road, and to Carlton villas (nos. 22-4, 1862), more in Turner's earlier Manor (Holcroft) road style[155].

By 1860, King Edward's road was built up eastwards as far as a block to the east of St Thomas's road; William Rayner's plots on the southern side taken in 1854 and 1858 producing double-fronted villas in the Butters manner, Butters himself by this time being at work on the Frampton estate and the Warburton estate west of Mare street. Norris's first building (with Rayner) on his second plot, under the 1859 agreement, is now 23-7 Ainsworth road, completed in the same year, originally as a Presbyterian hall and college, subsequently becoming a synagogue. Leases of the first Norris houses under this agreement, neighbouring the hall, were granted in 1860, and in the early years of the decade Norris's building grew steadily eastwards, to meet

Henry Bagge's building on the namesake estate[156].

King Edward's road was not fully dedicated to the public until the Henry Norris section, now Moulins road, was developed (1863-6). Thus it was that Benjamin Clarke could write in his old age of his memories of the prospect from the new South Hackney church in the 1850's, when he was in his thirties -

"I have a strong impression in my own mind that this road was laid out, as far as Shore place, years before its full dedication to the parish, and its bordering of houses, many of which are most substantial, well built, and really stylish residences, with good gardens, especially on the northern side, at their back. The road looked fairly levelled, although the grass had so overgrown it, that it looked part of the field itself..."[157]

After 1856, when Currey produced a further survey for the Governors, the focus of building on the estate moved northwards to the site of Loddiges' nursery in Well street, which closed in that year, its famous palm trees being carried in dignified procession all the way to their new home at the Crystal Palace. From 1858, Stanley road and Loddiges road were built up, and from 1860 Darnley and Devonshire roads, by various builders including Butters, James Harman, E.B. Winter and Abel Pilgrim, until mid-decade[158].

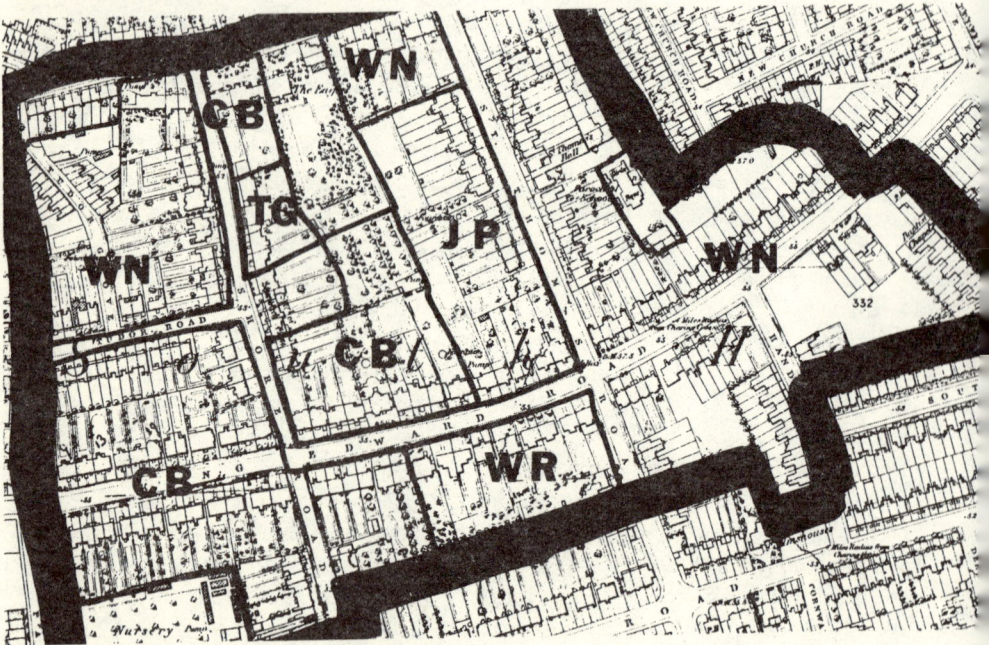

St Thomas's Hospital estate: building agreements
Key
   WN - William Norris; CB - Charles Butters; TG - T. P. Glaskin; JP - John Pearson; WR - William Rayner

The Suburban Village: Brookfield road

The 3 acre field lying between Grove street lane (Victoria Park road east) and
Cassland road, to the east of the Cass property, came on the market in 1854.
Whatever circumstances of the Mann family gave rise to this, it can never have
seemed a coherent part of their estate, being divided from their other Hackney Wick
property by the Mills family land to the east.

The purchaser was a body called the Suburban Villa and Village Association.
Relatively little is known about the association, save that it had characteristics similar
to the large family of mutual benefit building societies operating around mid-century,
and a majority of those identified as being associated with it as subscribers seem to
have had some connection with the textile trade, whether as tailors, clothiers or
drapers, although a baker and a "fruit broker" are also to be found. The society's aims
have to be inferred from its title. Apart from Hackney, the only known scene of its
operations was at Sydenham, near the Crystal Palace.

Its plan, drawn up by or in the office of the surveyor William Snooke, was that
these 3 Hackney acres were to be divided into 41 plots, for which advertisements were
published in May 1855. To each of these a value, expressed by a number of shares, was
allocated. These values ranged from 16 shares for a detached villa at the southern and
north-western entrances to the development, to 8 shares for a semi-detached, with
several variations in between to take account of location and aspect[159].

Before selecting a plot, a subscriber had to have fully paid up the prescribed
number of shares, which cost £25 each, and for which a minimum monthly payment
of 4 shillings and 2 pence (21p) was required. Thus the grandest villa - the surviving
one of two is Innall Cottage, no. 333 Victoria Park road, recently altered and
extended - would have cost £400 in share subscriptions, plus £130 for the land. The
humblest - the cheapest wedge of the intended terraced row on the north eastern
corner, fronting Cassland road and the cottages of Silk mill row - would have been
£200 plus £40. Each of numbers 2 and 4, which being built in 1856 were the earliest
on the site, would have been £250 plus £75. These sums were estimated by the
organisers as about 60 per cent of the cost of the house and land, but members were
free to put up something more expensive should they be able and willing to do so. The
remainder of the building cost they tended to raise privately, on mortgage.

On the basis of a ten year subscription cycle to work up the necessary entitlement
to build, however, it was hardly surprising that take-up was relatively slow. A number
of members recorded as having been allocated plots never seem to have followed
through to the building stage. The association's Secretary, Nicholas Thorpe, himself
subscribed for five plots in 1856/7. This he was only entitled to do if there were no
other members unsatisfied, as the basic rule was one plot per member. One or two of
the first built houses, such as no. 13, were set in substantial grounds, complete with

stable, as a result[160].

All the activities of societies building through subscriptions were affected by inflation in the mid-1850's, and numerous building and land societies faltered. Whether or not directly or indirectly on this account, by 1863 this association had given up its City offices and disappeared from view. By this time about 19 plots had been sold, all but a couple in the earliest years of development, 1856 and 1857. Other allocations, if they were taken up, do not seem to have resulted in development, whether on a one-house-per-plot basis or more luxuriously. Numbers 2 to 8 were first, and number 35, recently rescued from ruin, were all built much as the initial layout had envisaged; the plots for 10 and 12 were also sold at an early date, with numbers 13, 21 and 31 all being in occupation by the end of the 1860's. Building was never completed according to plan, with one site never developed and a multiple plot (now flats) on the west side accommodating, about 1890, the Tyndale Primitive Methodist Church[161].

It was presumably never intended, in any event, that any architectural uniformity should be achieved by the development, although the share money appears to have been deployed, in the early cases where development was contemporary, through the same builders, James Raby of the Hackney road, and Thomas Gardner of King's Cross. The builders of two houses on the Grove street lane frontage, Adams and son from Ealing, came from further afield than any other identified South Hackney builders[162].

If from the name of their association the promoters may be taken to have aspired to a village idyll in a London suburb, the result of their approach was perfectly consistent with the haphazard quality of the characteristic English village, as certainly no uniformity resulted. Whether the rural aspiration was consistent with the character of neighbouring development is another matter. Silk mill row was poor quality housing, and of some age; as recently as 1847 the condition of its sewerage arrangements had caused the deaths of the children of one of its residents. Cassland road was already laid out; the Hackney brook, a foul stream by mid century, was a field or so away to the north, beyond the small houses George Hedger was about to put up. These last were certainly not such as would have lent colour to a rural fantasy[163].

The most remarkable comparison, however, is with the development by the St Pancras, Marylebone and Paddington Freehold Land Society on the Hickling estate around the same time, where despite development which was similarly spread over many years, almost complete uniformity of design was achieved. But equally with that development, Brookfield road has its own special charm, situated as it is on a curve of a hill, and if the result is not exactly rural, the estate has a pleasing idiosyncrasy which make the earliest houses in particular worthy of careful conservation.

A respectable neighbourhood: Warneford and Fremont streets

Zillah Hickling, owner of the small estate lying to the south and west of the St Thomas's land, south of what became King Edward's road, died in 1845, her estate being divided within her family. Some ten years later the largest part, the orchard and small garden that lay behind the Mare street frontage of her house, was sold (after access from this enclosed area to Victoria park road had been negotiated with the Cass trustees) to a body who were, in 1855, much in the business of buying up small estates on the developing fringes of London: the St Pancras, Marylebone and Paddington Freehold Land Society[164].

This body had been formed in 1849 for the purpose of enlarging the Whig vote in Parliament. Following the Parliamentary Reform Bill in 1832, the franchise was extended to all adult males owning freehold land with an annual rental value of more than 40 shillings (£2) in the country, or house property worth £10 annually in the boroughs. This having created the incentive, there sprang up societies whose purpose was to increase the partisan vote by encouraging moderately affluent sympathisers - typically small tradesmen in the central districts where they had little prospect of acquiring freehold property - to become owners slightly further afield. These societies came later in London than elsewhere, and though the Whigs led the Tories followed, to the extent that by 1860 parts of north London were peppered by small estates being laid out in the name of a new type of voter-landowner, of both persuasions.

In several ways the societies worked like the early building societies; a subscriber would, by buying enough shares, or subscribing the required amount, become entitled to purchase a plot of land, often allocated by ballot. (Once he had received his allocation, of course, there was no way of ensuring that the subscriber stuck to his original political allegiance.) Because of legal limitations on landholding by building societies, however, where building finance was allied to land allocation a separate body would be formed for this purpose.

The St Pancras society, which claimed to be London's first, was established by a group of gentlemen in Camden Town (including two builder-surveyors, Rowe and Timpson), who obtained as their chairman Sir Benjamin Hall, the energetic M.P for St Marylebone. (He was promoter of the Bill which resulted in the 1855 reform of London local government by creating the new system of vestries and boards of works, but is more lastingly commemorated by the name given to the Westminster bell whose re-hanging he supervised - Big Ben.)[165]

Like the developers of Brookfield road, the Society was restricted by its rules as to the number of plots any one shareholder might take on an estate, in its case to two - being in the business of maximising the number of voters. The first allocation, at Lismore Circus in Kentish Town, had been a runaway success, but with the mid-decade recession allocations slowed down somewhat. The earliest developments were notable for the ideological content of the names given to streets laid out by the society: Franchise, Reform and Freehold streets distinguished (briefly) one of the developments at Holloway, and Hampden, Cromwell and Rupert streets the other. By contrast, the Hackney estate resorted unoriginally to royalty and rurality (Victoria street, Gotha street and Park street), leading inevitably to re-naming when later in the century the Metropolitan Board of Works set about rationalising many such overworked names.

By 1856 the society claimed eleven sites and 2,650 members, and had allocated all plots on its existing estates. In 1857 it formed its own building society, in which anybody might invest, but from which only Land Society members might borrow. Some of its public statements have to be taken however with a degree of scepticism. In 1857 it noted with apparent satisfaction -

"On all the estates building is now progressing. The Gospel Oak, Long Lands, Upper Holloway, Notting Hill and Hackney, have attracted the vigilant eye of the speculative builder, and on each substantial dwellings are erected, good business premises built, and respectable neighbourhoods fast forming, securing to the industrial classes a habitation and a home; whilst the allottee, of a more calculating turn, happily enjoys the incoming of a ground rent from £4 to £5 yearly, for the small outlay of £30 to £40, and paid back by the simple and easy means of one shilling weekly."[166]

A sum of this kind might buy a plot, but it did not build a house; builders would have to be found to give such a ground rent, or building financed through separate borrowing. Ground rent of £4 or £5 would have been the going rate from a Victoria Park road builder for a spacious villa; it was unlikely to be matched for the Society's frontages of 17' 10".

The first allocations on the Hackney estate were made in 1855, and, curiously, considering the claims made by the Society as to competition for allocations, in some cases resulted in the allocation of three plots per subscriber. There were 65 different purchasers, for between £39 and £50 per plot, some plots being taken in the names of children. The point being to obtain a vote, not all the new landowners rushed into building; indeed in the economic climate of the mid-1850's building activity was hampered by the scale of withdrawals, which may account for the difference between the claims of the publicity and the actuality[167].

Several of the Society's estates were very slow to fill up with houses, particularly those established in mid-decade. Many of the plots on the Wembley estate remained undeveloped and were let for grazing, while others, as the Society's publicity indicates, might serve as allotments. On the Hackney estate also building development was slow. Houses were put up apparently at random; applications to the vestry for the connection of drains into the sewers (constructed by Rowe and Timpson at the expense of each plotholder) proceeded at an average of two a year, the builders being individuals not otherwise known to be active in South Hackney: James Haynes,

William Feast, Joseph Dabell and Silas Honeywill, the latter also building (on a larger scale) on Englefield and Southgate roads at Dalston. Only Feast was himself a plotholder, and in fact went into residence on the estate.

By 1870 some 60 houses had been built; approximately a quarter of the acreage was undeveloped. 30 King Edward's road (now gone) occupied a triple plot, and the two-plot rule had been deployed to allow a side garden to one of the terraced houses on the east side of Warneford street; it would shortly thereafter give rise to 26 King Edward's road (later the Ayahs' Home). In the case of the Society's developments the random pattern of building had nothing to do with any ballotting process, as (although ballotting for places on an estate) they insisted on a strict first come first serve basis for site allocations. It must therefore result from the haphazard intentions of the various subscribers[168].

The Society may have had hopes of pushing the western spur of Warneford street, which now as on their original plan ends in a dead end, through to Mare street. The planned layout envisaged longer east-west terraces, the western end of the street blocked by a brick wall. Marmaduke Matthews, the auctioneer and Wick road developer whose own house (Cambridge lodge) bounded the Society's estate to the west at this point, may well have been known to be prepared to build on his own backyard. But although Matthews was laying out a side street, more or less on the line of the Society's east-west spur road, no deal resulted, and in 1856 he built a pair of large semi's, which he called Cambridge lodge villas, set so far back from Mare street that their back wall formed the Society's boundary. Eventually the Society's estate layout was revised, two houses short of its original number, and Warneford street ends not as a brick wall but as a completely returned frontage[169].

The conditions of sale restricted building to houses only, and required conformity with the Society's planned elevations. In spite of the two grander detached villas fronting King Edward's road, and the single builder's yard that filled an unusually narrow plot in Warneford street, it is evident that before the removal of cornices there was indeed a high degree of consistency in the street elevations throughout the estate, the quality of which has been recently and belatedly recognised in conservation area status. It is not now easy to tell whether the handful of variations in the rooflines on the estate date from first building or later alteration. As all sales were freehold, there was no common builder and development was to all intents and purposes random. The uniformity - taken together with the variation of height achieved, and what must have been, as the years passed, an increasingly unfashionable design - is therefore quite remarkable. There is almost total consistency in the doorcases and segmented window arches, and even relative internal consistency, as between the different street frontages, of response to the problem of a fourth storey.

It is tempting to attribute the design to the surveyor Charles Poland, who was not only a prime mover in the Society but the first allottee on the estate itself, taking three plots (including those for 14 and 16 King Edward's road) but there is no hard evidence. The standard of design is however higher than on some of the Society's other completed estates, which are plain and inoffensive but lack the charm of detail given by window pediments, quoins and cornices to Warneford and Fremont streets. Some also lack the consistency[170].

Also striking, as already noted, is the contrast in the approach taken to laying out this small estate with that on the Brookfield road estate of the Suburban Villa and Village association less than half a mile away. Both societies operated through subscriptions; both sold their plots freehold (in the case of the St Pancras society, this was, of course, an article of faith). But the concept of the community being created could not have been more different in each case. The nature of the vision that Brookfield road was to embody is quite clear from the association's name: the concept was very much that of the suburb as country village, and may well have been an attempt at a self-starting suburban community. In the interests of maximising Whig voters, the St Pancras society, on the other hand, brought to the developing suburb an enclave that was as thoroughly urban in its conception as were its estates in Gospel Oak and Notting Hill. In its own way, it is as much London in the country as Thomas Pickering's Hackney terrace of sixty years earlier. And while it is clear that most of the Freehold Land Society residents were not owner-occupiers, the position in relation to Brookfield road's earliest years is uncertain.

There was one other development of significance on Hickling land, and that was equally urban in style - so much so that nos. 4-12 King Edward's road look as if they have strayed to South Hackney in mistake for Knightsbridge or South Kensington. Built in 1860, originally as a row of six ("Northumberland houses"), on the portion of the estate that fell some fifteen years previously to Jonathan Hickling, an ironmonger in Hoxton[171], their builder is as yet unknown. They defy the more typical South Hackney builder's dilemma, whether to build high or to build wide, a dilemma that was by 1860 beginning to resolve itself in favour of the terrace rather than the villa; but on a scale that would have dismayed the architect of the Northumberland houses, destined to remain unique.

The late 1850's

The Cass estate

With the laying out of Victoria Park road dormant for the time being, the Cass trustees faced the inflationary years following 1855 in the knowledge that they needed to seize the initiative if competition from other, perhaps more fortunately placed estates was not to edge them out of the running in what was becoming a highly competitive housing market.

There was little building activity in the second half of the 1850's, except on the northern part of the estate, where Robert Kitteridge and Charles Lefever began developing Cassland road eastwards of Bradstock road, and the frontages of Terrace road were developed, by individual, small-scale local builders, as well as by Page and by Gillespy[172].

The Cass trustees had developed a sophisticated and tailor-made system for managing their estate and its development. In the early days of the estate the surveyor, Jesse Gibson, a resident of Grove street, had like the trustees' legal adviser, Jeremiah Bentham (father of Jeremy) given his services on a fee basis, as and when required. Gibson's successor in title, George Wales, was salaried, whatever other fees he may have been able to earn from executing designs for prospective developers, and ran the day-to-day business of the estate very effectively from the estate office next to his home at the west end of Hackney terrace, imposing, as we have seen, some degree of uniformity on development on his employers' land, and encouraging fashionable diversity on that of their neighbours.

In 1855 the charity's Registrar, John Clark, had volunteered that his own fee be reduced, so much of his routine business of drawing up agreements and leases having been handed over to the surveyor. The latter took stock, and identified that his office entailed acting as surveyor, receiver of rents, and clerk of works: in order to discharge the design element of his duties he had to employ two drawing office assistants out of his own pocket. Prices had risen significantly in the previous couple of years; and evidently the standardisation of leases had saved the estate the costs of involving the Registrar. He therefore claimed £350 annually, on the basis that the estate office continued to open throughout the week; he was willing to reduce this to £300 if the office was only open on three days. For this the trustees willingly settled. Its corporate learning period all but over, the Cass estate began what might be called the production line phase of its development[173].

For this George Wales held the key. He suggested, in April 1856, that it would be expedient to apply to the directors of the North London (or "Camden Town") railway, for a station at Hackney Wick, on the line (opened in 1850) between Camden Town and the Docks. He was accordingly instructed to do so, and to find out the "conditions (if any) required to induce the Directors to construct such a station".

There appear to have been none; and if Wales's approach was the first the Directors had heard of the idea they must have moved with what seems to the consumer of modern bureaucracy to be astonishing speed, as the station, alluringly named Victoria Park, was opened in July of that year[174].

There was no direct link from this station to the City until, in 1865, the line to Broad street was opened; until then access to the City required a change at Stepney onto the Fenchurch street line. The opening of railway access must however, as Wales will have intended, have played a part in the later successful marketing of the north east corner of the estate.

Frampton Park

The intense period of South Hackney's development was poised to start. Charles Butters and T. P. Glaskin, builder/ developers of the St Thomas's estate and unique in South Hackney as being apparently unaffected by the recession of the late 1850's, began building in partnership on the estate of the late Dr Algernon Frampton in 1856, arranging for it to be laid out in sympathy with that part of the St Thomas's estate lying north of Well street, largely occupied by the famous Loddiges nursery until that year. The Cass trustees, on whose estate large scale development was still to hang fire for several years, with only a handful of new leases granted each year before 1862, "hoped to make arrangements with them, for improvement of the property of the neighbourhood"[175]. This seems to have involved, in Wales's scheme of things, a new road to join Loddiges road with the foot of Cassland road, and had as its principal object the elimination of much of the ancient and run-down property around the old Prior's House. This did not take place; indeed it did not lie in the power of the Frampton executors to deliver.

It was however - as may well have been the fear of the Cass trustees - the Frampton estate that set the seal on the style of development that was to be the staple in South Hackney on the remaining development land. More spacious than anything hitherto built on the fringe of South Hackney, they were nevertheless a complete departure from the detached and semi-detached villas, or large terraces, favoured in Cassland crescent, Victoria park road or King Edward's road. Solid, unadorned two or three storey houses with back projections almost the length of the main body of the house, they ran in unornamented terraces of twenty and upwards, the houses in Glaskin road and the west side of Frampton park road having small front gardens, and the rest none. To the eastern end of the estate, adjoining the old nucleus of Well street which sank, as the century progressed, to become a recognised slum, the houses and gardens were smaller than on the main Frampton park and Glaskin roads.

The leases, for which Rayner was once again Butters's sub-contractor, were first granted in 1858, and timed to expire some 99 years after the letting of the building agreement. The estate was complete by 1860; the larger houses of the northern St Thomas's estate with which it was co-ordinated not until 1865[176].

Homer Road

A further development of terraced houses, although on a much smaller scale, took place in Homer Road. The name given to this road, despite local theory, has nothing to do with Homerton, but everything to do with John James Homer, wine merchant of Finch lane, Cornhill, and vestryman of South Hackney in the early 1850's; and his brother, William Richard Homer, with whom he was publican at the Dolphin in Mare street.

In or about 1858, J. J.Homer took a lease, probably a building lease, for a period of not more than 80 years, from the freeholder (J. R. Mills, M P for Wycombe, and son of Samuel Mills of Russell square, who had died in 1847) of a triangle of land immediately north of the north-eastern tip of Victoria Park and east of the Suburban Villa and Village Association's development at Brookfield road. This like its neighbouring land was isolated from the landowner's other local holdings further north and east[177].

Homer developed the central section of the land himself, as two rows of terraced houses facing each other east and west, letting the eastern terrace to his brother. The northern segment, two terraces of 18 in all on Park Street, Wick Road, were sub-let to the developer James Harman (then at the beginning of his career in Hackney). There is nothing left now of either development.

The rest was sub-let to T. P. Glaskin, veteran of the St Thomas's and Frampton estate developments, who in September 1858 made a successful proposal to the Cass trustees for 3 parcels of neighbouring land at Hackney Wick, for use as a brickfield, in connection with neighbouring development. This was the only proposal of its kind ever accepted by that estate, and they must have been influenced not only by the lack of alternatives but the situation of the site on the extreme north east of their holdings.

Glaskin was very slow to develop either of his Hackney Wick sites, although from 1857 the laying out of the Frampton estate proceeded apace, no doubt with Hackney Wick bricks, and he was similarly active on the more centrally situated Warburton estate at London Fields. He sub-contracted the building of numbers 347-369 Victoria park road (Homer terrace) to E.J. Willmott, nos. 371-9 being later infilling. Glaskin also built the then neighbouring Elephant and Castle pub - an "architectural monstrosity", according to Millicent Rose[178] - which was taken by Messrs J. and W. S. Holt of the Marine Brewery, Ratcliff (an advertisement for whose "entire" stout survives in the parapet to the Warburton Arms, in Mare street, another area where Willmott, in addition to Glaskin, was active in the late 1850's)[179].

On the Cass frontage of Grove street lane Glaskin's sub-contractor H. R. Allen began in 1862 the eastern segment of the long series of terraces, including other builders' work further west, which began with Bagge's building opposite the then Queen's Hotel and were known as Grove villas. Of Glaskin's frontage on Victoria Park road nos. 309-11 are the only survivals[180].

In the meantime, development elsewhere on the Cass estate consisted of the completion of the western end of Victoria Park road, where most of the remaining Cass land was taken by Hugh Eastman on 90 year leases, his offer for 99 having been turned down. Nos. 89-95, which he called Somerset villas, have already been noted. Nos. 69 to 79, of the same years (1860-2) are distinguished, if nothing else, by the curiously alphabetical, building site approach to their names as given in the leases: they were Albany, Buckingham, Carlton, Dumbarton, Eastbourne and Fairlight villas respectively[181]. It is a pity that the names incised on the porticos do not all survive, because the name given to site B paid a unique compliment to Eastman's builder and clerk of works, Thomas Buckingham - one that the developer might have forgone had the name been something less aristocratic, such as Bagge or Borton, as he so clearly forwent it himself in his own house, three doors away. The alphabet continued with Gordon villas (57-67), Harley villas (53-5), and, on Norris territory, Kendal terrace (147-201)[182].

There was intermittent letting of sites on the north-eastern section, particularly in Bentham road and the northern section of Bradstock road, surrounding the ropeworks, and on the adjacent portion of Cassland road, where until he ran into difficulties and had to be relieved from his agreement Robert Kitteridge was endeavouring to confront the spectre of Hackney bay on the estate's behalf. In Bentham road, the brothers Innes, merchants of Mincing lane, financed in 1860/2 the first range of surviving terraced houses (nos. 4 to 28) with their intriguing but attenuated Gothic details, on the south side next to George Day's pub and outbuildings (the Kenton Arms) of 1854. The brothers had undertaken to build some 12 to 13 more, which undertaking they did not fulfil during the remainder of the decade, although the estate was sufficiently prepared to tolerate their preference for what they called their "wholesale" way of dealing in land that another agreement for land in Bentham road (to build the best class of houses that the land would bear, in the estimation of the Cass surveyor) was negotiated in April-June 1867[183].

Frampton House .1867

The Norris estate

During 1850, the last year of H H Norris's life, the basic plan for eventual development of at least the western half of his Hackney estate had been more or less settled by the Currey plan, on which St Thomas's and, from the evidence of Benjamin Clarke, the Norrises themselves had acted, by laying out King Edward's road westwards to the boundary of their land with the Hospital's.

Since 1846, if not earlier, H. H. Norris's heir and only child, Henry, had been to all intents and purposes in charge of running the estate, although, like several of his forefathers, he had removed himself to some distance from his parental home, living first at Wroxton, Oxfordshire before settling at Swalcliffe, near Banbury[184].

In 1843, soon after the acquisition of the Currie land, the plan for the new church for South Hackney was commissioned from E. C. Hakewill[185].

The Norris almshouses

Henrietta Norris, the Rector's wife, survived her husband by nearly four years; there was no attempt at development of the estate during her lifetime, or indeed for some years afterwards. The only building during this period was of almshouses, founded as a memorial to the late Rector, and initiated by subscription amongst the parishioners. These consisted of four houses, designed by Charles Parker, later surveyor to the Bedford estate, in a Gothic style reminiscent of 1-3 Church Crescent. They were built on a prominent site, but one chosen not to interfere with the integrity of later development, on the north side of Victoria park road, west of what became Handley road[186].

The subscription had failed to meet its target, there being insufficient money raised to build the six houses originally intended, leading to the abandonment of an innovative design by Hakewill. Indeed the project might not have materialised without a gift of the land from Henry Norris, and a contribution of £300 from his mother. In part the shortfall seems to have arisen because of competition with another fund, begun by the diocesan authorities, "to advance one or other of those great objects to which the life of Mr Norris was devoted". To the trustees of this fund, who undoubtedly had in mind the involvement of "the energetic old man of Grove street" with the church school movement and the Society for Promoting Christian Knowledge, the object of poor relief in South Hackney was evidently insufficiently great.

The almshouses, opened in 1857, were to house "widows, or unmarried women of good character", who were also members of the Church of England and resident in South Hackney. Some belated redress was envisaged for the long-standing plight of the widows of Monger's almsmen, who were to have preference amongst equally eligible candidates.

The first building agreements

Market conditions in the late 1850's, after the death of Henrietta, can have afforded Henry Norris little incentive to build on his Hackney estate; and it may be, as is discussed below, that he was seeking a price far higher than the market would bear. Either way, in the early 1860's the tide had begun to turn. Most notably, large villas on the Crown land south of Victoria Park road were being built and, even more to the point, finding tenants. Early in 1862, he achieved the realignment of Grove street, which had been in his mind at least since 1846. The old highway had run almost due north, emerging at the east end of the church; it was re-formed somewhat to the west, on an alignment which neatly bisected the church's island site, and two old footpaths across the fields to King Edward's road were stopped up[187].

The Currey plan, somewhat extended towards the east, and minus the rather grandiose circuses that were its most striking feature, was nevertheless the basis of the layout that was about to be put into execution, superintended by Currey himself[188].

Preparations for Handley, Speldhurst and Southborough roads having already begun in the spring, in mid-summer Henry Norris concluded formal building agreements for the construction of roads on the portion of his estate west of Grove street, to a density only fractionally greater than Currey's 1850 layout had proposed. The Victoria Park road frontage, for example, originally set out by Currey in four terraces of six houses each, was taken by Hugh Eastman, who at that time was completing his infill terrace at nos. 89-95. Eastman's Kendal terrace (nos. 147 to 201), to each of the four components of which one house was added to the original six, went swiftly into construction, the first terrace being complete by October 1862[189].

Eastman's position as one of the prime developers in the area may have enabled him to drive a harder bargain than his rivals, as he was able to secure here, as on the Cass estate, a 90 year term. For other development Norris went to Henry Bagge, a bricklayer by trade, who had begun in a small way in Glaskin road on the Frampton estate as a sub-contractor to Charles Butters. Here, with his partner Robert Morley, also a builder in Glaskin road, he negotiated a substantial contract (the exact terms of which do not survive) with Norris for the western part of the estate, on 80 year terms from June 1862. Thus it was the partnership of Bagge and Morley who were responsible for the building of Speldhurst road (1862/3), and the western part of Southborough road (1863/4), together with both eastern and western frontages on Lauriston road (1865). Morley himself, with a sub-contractor, took most of the leases at the eastern end of King Edward's road (now Moulins road), in the twelve months beginning in April 1865; by this time Henry Bagge was heavily engaged on his own account on the Cass estate[190].

To the developers, ground rents for the Victoria park road frontage, after the customary period of grace, were settled at £6, and on the same principle an identical sum was asked for King Edward's road. In the hinterland, the rate to the developer seems to have been set at £5, save for prime sites on Lauriston road. Rarely on the western sector of the Norris estate was a lease granted directly to an investor or prospective occupant. Bagge, or Morley, or the partners jointly, took the bulk of them, a handful going to any of their nine or ten sub-contractors, but principally to John Scholtes and William Lavers. It may be that the partnership chose to front-load their ground rents, because between September 1863 and the following spring leases in Southborough road and the very end of Speldhurst road were granted at a maximum of one pound, occasionally less. The eastern side of Lauriston road was not completed until 1867, in which year the remaining Bagge and Morley leases in Southborough Road (nos. 49 & 51) were granted.

Bagge himself moved in to no. 1 Speldhurst road. This road was named as early as spring 1862, but the naming of the other western roads caused more difficulty. To Benjamin Bishop, not alone among the sub-contractors, Southborough road was known as Merrimac road (alluding to a naval incident during the American Civil war in 1862), and Bagge and Morley themselves had initially referred to it as Suffolk road[191]. No doubt Henry Norris asserted his own views, renaming this, as well as all but one of the remaining streets after villages near the country estate at Lankington Green, Speldhurst, near Tunbridge Wells, which had belonged to his uncle and subsequently his cousin, both called Baden Powell (the latter, who had died in 1860, being Savilian professor of geometry at Oxford and father of the founder of the Boy Scouts). The exception was of course Banbury Road, which compliments Henry Norris's own country seat at Swalcliffe Park.

The French Hospital

Henry Norris was equally ready to let the eastern segment of his estate, and the first in the field were the trustees of the French Hospital, formally known as the "Hospital for Poor French Protestants and their Descendants residing in Great Britain". This, the almshouses (and originally the infirmary) of London's community of Huguenots, had been founded in 1716 in Bath street, Finsbury, but by the 1830's both the building and its neighbourhood had ceased to be suitable for the purpose. After twenty years of making do and mending, and some exploratory discussions with landowners of possible new sites, in 1857 a move was recognised as inevitable, and the Directors sought "a more suitable building in a healthy and a more agreeable locality"[192].

The Hospital authorities quite early conceived a preference for the area of Victoria Park for a new building, not least because of the closeness of Hackney to the weaving districts from which the hospital inmates were drawn, and the fact that good quality villas were going up in the neighbourhood. This preference was far from unanimous, the dissentients being no doubt those of the directors who did not themselves live in the vicinity. The inmates were consulted as to their preference: only 10 of the 53 were adamant that they preferred to remain on "the old spot"; the special committee appointed to consider the subject reported that "amongst those who prefer the present locality are the inmates of no.6 - the disorderly ward - some of whom are the most troublesome in the hospital"[193].

The awkward squad did not prevail, and sites as far afield as Holloway, Snaresbrook and Thornton Heath were considered, as well as land in the disposal of T. P. Glaskin abutting the Warburton estate at London Fields. After much deliberation, in July 1861 the directors finally settled on the neighbourhood of Victoria Park.

The relative merits of the various sites in the area had been explored over some years. In 1855 the Hospital had been wooed, and then hustled, by George Wales, who had heard that they had made enquiries of Henry Norris, and tried to alarm them as to his rival's likely price. He himself was offering 20 acres of former market garden north of Grove street lane, on an 80 year lease at an annual rent of £100; the land seems to have been part of that subsequently taken by Glaskin, and did not appeal to the Hospital, as fronting north onto Cassland road not the park. Even when a more acceptable plot was on offer, the Hospital not being ready to act, Wales responded: "I do not think [the Cass trustees] would be willing to reopen the question at any future time. I am sure a liberal proposition has been put before you...Mr Norris and others who hold land in this neighbourhood consider £2,000 per acre is the value!"[194]

Indeed there do not seem to have been any subsequent approaches to the Cass estate. Pennethorne was approached for Crown land, but the response was that objection was taken to buildings other than private dwelling houses on Park land - a policy that must have been adopted after the building of the Chest Hospital on the Bethnal Green side. Thomas Natt, owner of the finger of land at the junction of Grove street lane and what is now Wetherell road, replied bluntly that he was waiting for the land value to rise, and that "the fine frontage it has, which would be sufficient, I apprehend, for 40 or more houses at a very reasonable ground rent for each, would produce a saleable value far above what a hospital could afford to give for a site..." As early as 1859 the Norris land was identified as most suitable, although Henry Norris rejected out of hand the Hospital's initial preference for the site immediately to the south of the church[195].

In August 1861 the Hospital offered for a site immediately to the east of the memorial almshouses; Du Cane, Norris's agent (and distant cousin) had fixed the price at £1200 per acre. Finding however that the public footpath from Grove street to Shore place ran across the land adjoining, which they considered would be too intrusive, they settled instead for a site on the extreme east of Norris's land on which the Hospital was built, despite the continuing objections of Giraud, a leading member of the Hospital's building committee, to the length of time it took to travel to the site from central London, to the lack of cabs, and, looking eastwards, "several tall chimney shafts surrounding the Park belonging to manufactories that do not consume their own smoke"[196].

The site ultimately chosen was the estate's easternmost plot, next to Well street common, and extended to some three and a half acres (and the old gardeners' outbuildings belonging to the former mansion) once the Hospital had adopted Henry Norris's suggestion that it include some "fine trees of long standing". The Hospital took up the offer made in 1857 by R. L. Roumieu, co-architect of De Beauvoir and Milner Squares, who (along with S. S. Teulon) had long been a member of the rebuilding committee, to design the building without charge. Never lacking invention, he came up with a design which was described as "a French chateau of the age of Francis I".

His brief was to provide accommodation for 40 women and 20 men, preferably with no more than a half basement and ground and first floors, the building to be a T-shape with a chapel at the east end. The plans were approved in August 1863, a minor reduction being made in the women's accommodation to allow for a small infirmary ward. It had been intended that the Hospital's surveyor, Frederick Herring, should supervise the building, but he withdrew, not without pique, on account of Roumieu's involvement, so it seems that the work fell on the architect himself.

The tender of Langmire and Burge, for £17,086 (some £5,000 over the initial budget, partly on account of the addition of a lodge) was accepted, and after some trouble with untrapped drains had been put right, the builders handed the site over to the Hospital in June 1865. The Directors later recorded with satisfaction that "in the summer of that year the inmates of the Hospital were safely transferred to their new building in Victoria Park, where they and their successors enjoy, in increased comfort, the few declining years of a life which has generally been one of hard toil and privation."[197]

The eastern estate

Towards the end of 1863, when Bagge and Morley were keeping up with their commitments on the western estate, but only taking the leases in hand at a low ground rent, Norris looked elsewhere for a developer to take on the remainder of the eastern estate. Although evidently Bagge and Morley must, from their having taken leases of the eastern side of Lauriston road, and indeed 49-51 Southborough road, have had some expectation of continuing, by this time Bagge had also taken a large plot from the Cass trustees, and it may well have appeared to Henry Norris from this, and from the rate of completions slowing up on the existing contract, that his developer was over-extending himself. A successor he found in James Harman, an ironmonger of Hoxton, who was reaching the peak of his career as a building speculator across a wide swathe of London from Willesden (where he maintained a country residence) through Kilburn to Harman street in the Kingsland road. (It may be recalled that he had already dabbled in the Homer estate at Hackney Wick, and been active on the northern part of the St Thomas's estate.)[198]

Harman, like Eastman, managed to settle for 90 year terms, and took the whole of the remainder of Norris's eastern estate, including Church Crescent, on building lease from Christmas 1863. The remaining frontages along Grove street lane were ultimately let, in 1865, to their principal builders, Benjamin Bishop (nos. 203-207), formerly a sub-contractor from Bagge, Charles Cockerell and John Scholtes (variously, nos. 209-221) and William Turner (nos. 223-243), the latter being the veteran of Holcroft Road. Four master builders sub-contracted from Harman: Stephen Martin, in Groombridge and Penshurst roads, James Jarvis, in the central section of the site, James Fowell, on the west side of Banbury road; and William Turner. Turner's house, the Cedars in Banbury road, one of only two detached villas on the estate, was to become the home for some 17 years of the family of Dr T. J. Barnardo. The great philanthropist's removal to South Hackney was sponsored by his father-in-law, in the interests of a semi-rural upbringing for his grandchildren, sufficiently removed from the influences of the East End[199].

The entire estate was complete by the end of 1867. Harman himself took leases of a substantial portion of the estate, including much of the north side of Groombridge road and all of Banbury road (including the Penshurst arms, the estate's only public house). Although many of the remaining leases were taken by the builders themselves, the enterprise was more fortunate than Bagge's in the rate of direct lettings.

Despite the head leases being granted mostly to the developers and builders, the estate does not in the long run seem to have been short of investors in house property. The directors of the French Hospital itself, in 1886, bought the ground rents of 26-64 Penshurst road, abutting their own north boundary, and that of Lammas House adjoining, a fact until recently recognised in small iron plaques attached to the centre of each short terrace. And despite his noting a decline in value in Hackney property in the 1880's, one investor in ground rents and mortgages on the estate was the originator of it all: Henry Currey[200].

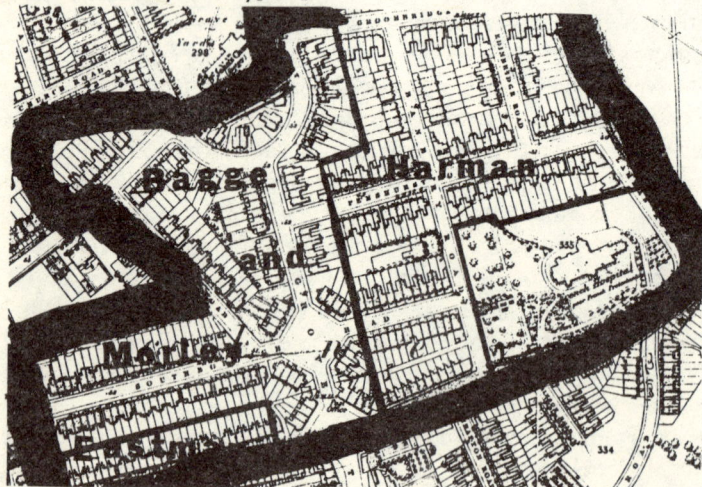

Norris estate: building agreements

Cass: the Final Phase

Exit George Wales

In 1860, the parish of St Botolph's, Aldgate mounted an assault on the management of Sir John Cass's charity, a repetition of an attempt to take control which had failed in the 1830's. Asserting that the founder's intention (which had been a vexed question since his death) was to benefit their City parish, they insisted on the submission to them of accounts; they appear to have been alarmed by reports that the trustees, who perceived an eventual need to replace the Aldgate schoolhouse, were contemplating removing the school to Hackney. The rumour was a highly specific one: the field at the eastern end of Hackney terrace was the supposed preferred site, and the model for rebuilding alleged to be the London Orphan Asylum at Clapton. The charity successfully asserted its accountability to the Charity Commissioners as opposed to the parish; the vestry committee, foiled, concentrated their attack on the personal dealings of the estate surveyor, George Wales, and the late Registrar, John Clark, in property interests derived from charity land[201].

It was a grapeshot attack. The lease to Clark of the backland of Blenheim cottages was attacked not only on its terms, as being for longer than the trustees were empowered to grant for non-building purposes; but because it benefited another charity, and not one of interest to St Botolph's. Much research was done into the surveyor's dealings in land. Some of the committee's findings seem misconceived: considering that Wales had been required to live on the estate, an attack on his lease of Cassland House seems ill-informed, given that no fault was found with the level of the rent; and an attack on him for involvement in management of parish charities scarcely sticks. Equally, the fact that Wales was investing private capital in funding some of the estate's building contractors (notably John Page) through mortgages is, as he himself asserted, of itself as consistent with the estate's interest as with his own. However, he also took assignment of leases post-development, from George Day, Thomas Gillespy and George Oldfield; and most of all the purchase at auction of some of Page's building land, which under the building agreement entitled the developer to leases on certification of the building by the estate surveyor. There remains, also, the suspicion that Clark had in his dealings with the trustees over the Terrace road and Cassland crescent properties received exceptionally favourable treatment.

Wales, in the knowledge that the vestry committee was deliberating was stung into seeking an assurance of his employers' confidence. Apart from his salary, he pointed out that the fees he had earned from his first ten years work for the estate had amounted to only £50. He wrote to them:

"You are aware what deep interest the late Mr Clark took in the affairs of the charity and in what self-sacrificing spirit he fulfilled the various buildings he undertook on the charity estate -

a spirit of emulation and similar desire for the interests of the charity induced me to do the same, and the result has proved a considerable pecuniary loss to both of us. I am not surprised at the loss, because I know it is difficult to build economically on a small scale, and that if fair ground rent is paid the result must be loss! The public will not pay the price of well built houses nor a remunerative percentage in the shape of rental in the Parish of Hackney...."

Although the trustees backed him up, and affirmed that everything he had done had been "in perfect good faith and greatly to the advantage of the charity", Wales may have nursed a grievance. Though some of his correspondence suggests a touchy, not to say a high-handed approach, he had expended his design abilities on the estate at large, and principally on Victoria park road (to a degree of success which even unsympathetic modern development has not totally impaired), only to suffer the frustrations of a sticky market. He had badgered the Crown estate to get on with their development job, to little or no immediate effect. He had experimented, perhaps given a freer hand, with more academic approaches to design when dabbling in speculation on neighbouring property, only to end up out of pocket and pilloried in the parish of St Botolph's [202].

During 1862 he showed further signs of restiveness. In 1856 he had obtained recognition in the form of a salary increase. In February of 1862, apparently the business had been so far further systematised as to enable him to ask for a revision of his salary to £260, on the understanding that he would attend at Hackney only on Saturdays. This seems to have been accepted without undue difficulty; but the probability is, nevertheless, that he was laying his plans for departure. The vestry committee had alleged he had undue influence over some of the trustees: it is now not clear whether after the criticism of his "trafficking" in their property he had retained the board's full confidence; but he was subsequently employed when in the late 1860's the schoolhouse was ultimately rebuilt[203].

In January 1863 he resigned his post, helping to draw up his successor's job description, and subsequently fighting a running battle with him over entitlement to certification fees on outstanding agreements. There was, however, to be no repetition of the vestry critique. Henry Fricker, who was appointed on a majority vote of a special meeting of trustees, found himself more circumscribed than Wales had been. He was required to find sureties for £1,000, and was expressly precluded from acting as surveyor or architect for building on the estate, his income from this source being restricted to certification fees under building agreements[204].

George Wales has left us with South Hackney's only visual pun. During 1862, the large site on the south side of Victoria park road, west of the present roundabout, had been taken by the Irish builder Thomas Fitzroy Kelly[205]. The whole block - the pub, the site for the neighbouring terrace acquired subsequently, and Kelly's own mansion, the double-fronted no. 128 - were to be named, although developed over the following decade, characteristically for that year after Alexandra of Denmark, who had just become engaged to be married to the heir to the throne. The Cass surveyor, in approving, and almost certainly himself creating, the designs for the building, took care to leave, almost as if it were his parting shot, his signature on the Princess Alexandra public house, on the corner of Lauriston road. The three feathers on the first floor keystones of this prominent building may be taken to allude not only to Alexandra's husband, but to another Prince of Wales.

Large scale development

It was during 1862 that the trend was consolidated towards large scale development of largely unindividuated smaller houses than the Cass estate had hitherto contemplated; it is tempting to point to the likely diminishing scope for architectural input as a feature in Wales's departure. In November of that year, when building on the Norris estate was well under way, R. E. Borton offered the Cass trustees an agreement for a minimum of 50 houses, south of Victoria Park road and west of Grove street. This formed the basis for his development of Rutland, Redruth and Derby roads, in association with Joseph Lucas and Mark Bean, during 1862-5. Borton's status as prime developer on the neighbouring Crown land no doubt assisted his successful bid, negotiated at a careful meeting, for a 90-year term at a ground rent of £150, with a minimum of £4 allocated to each house. Each was to have an annual value of not less than £24, and letting would be in groups of up to six if required. By dint of extensive sub-contracting, this agreement was completed by 1866[206].

During 1862, Eastman was completing his infill of Somerset villas (89-95 Victoria Park road) on a similar term; the Innes brothers were building 16 to 28 Bentham road, having already developed the terrace to the west; and T. P. Glaskin was at long last completing houses, which he called Grove villas (309-327 Victoria Park road) along the main frontage of the brickfield he had taken in 1858. Building, in the hands of Philip Meldrum, was also progressing on the limited frontage in St Thomas's (Ainsworth) road that belonged to the Cass estate.

In 1863, progress was made by the estate towards the completion of building on the fields between the eastern arm of Victoria park road and Cassland road east of Gascoyne road. The first major building agreement in this area was settled in September of that year, with Henry Bagge, who was already heavily involved on the western part of the Norris estate and who, had, apparently, shed his erstwhile partner, Robert Morley. Under this agreement (whose "propriety" gave the Cass trustees some pause) Bagge undertook to build houses, on 80 year terms, on what became Harrowgate road[207].

The cause of the trustees' anxiety are not clear; the rent, at £230, compared favourably with that available elsewhere; but their misgivings were borne out. Bagge agreed to build 80 houses at a rate of at least 20 a year, and from an early point his lack of progress and building standards caused concern. He was also found to be excavating excessively for sewers, in order to sell the sand and gravel. In 1865, he engaged at least 8 different sub-contractors, each of whom took between 2 and 12 houses to finish, resulting in a patchwork of underleases and assignments. Only one of these, Evan Lewis, seems to have established himself sufficiently to surface in the area as a contractor on his own account, notably in Kenton cottages on the west side of Kenton road[208].

About this time, William Redgrave took a building lease of the site at the south east corner of the newly laid out roundabout on Victoria park road, at its junction with Grove street, and swiftly built it up with shops and houses over on both the Victoria park road and Grove street (Lauriston road) frontages: he was later to go on and build houses and shops, now demolished, at the junction of Kenton road and Wick road. At the same time, to the west, Cintra villas, on the site of the present Regency Court, were being built[209].

But the most important agreement was that in the following year, 1864, with John Wright, a builder with premises at West street, near the Triangle, who undertook to build not less than 150 houses on the site bounded by Bagge's Harrowgate road on the west and Glaskin's brickfield on the east[210]. Thus were conceived Annis and Christie roads (honouring, once again, past treasurers of Sir John Cass's charity) to be built by Wright's numerous sub-contractors in a style not noticeably different from Harrowgate road. That Glaskin's ultimate development on his brickfield (over which the Cass trustees had retained little control, leases being granted by the developer himself) is again little different is scarcely surprising, in that Wright was employed as sub-contractor to fulfil what remained of the delayed agreement, probably sub-letting to his own contractor R. T. Banks. This development, part of which was originally called Dagmar terrace in honour of the Princess of Wales's sister the Duchess of Fife, was later renamed Danesdale road.

During 1865, Wright's development seems to have been successful in attracting early investors, and proved even more so in the following year, although a significant proportion of the leases were granted to his sub-contractors, notably H. R. Allen. Meanwhile in Harrowgate road, Bagge was having difficulty. His initial lack of progress he put down to bad climatic conditions. However, once they had moved in, the residents of the road were vociferous about its unmade state, and difficult interviews with the Cass trustees failed to resolve the matter amicably. Neither Bagge nor T. F. Kelly (who had put himself on the wrong side of the trustees by building stabling on the back land behind the Alexandra pub without permission) were readily acceptable to the estate from this time on as prospective building developers, although Kelly was ultimately restored to favour, securing in 1873 the agreement for 19-35 Bramshaw road[211].

Bagge's Victoria park road frontage, nos. 253-261, by virtue of gratuitous alteration, now disguises the difference between his plain pattern-book, early Victorian style and the more florid triple-windows or decorated columns adopted by the neighbouring developers to the east.

Throughout the rest of the decade, and beyond, the corner of land south east of the Lauriston road roundabout was developed on 80-year building leases, largely by W. B. Dyer, of Tredegar road, Bow, with finance from brick and lime merchants Robert and Thomas Wright. The first agreements, for Minson and Shafton roads, were let in 1866. Dyer also had control of Ruthven street and the nearby Lauriston road frontage, begun in 1871 and completed the following year[212].

The northern estate

At the same time, the northern part of the Cass estate was being built up. In 1864, the first building was achieved in Queen Anne's road. This was no.2, which makes it surprising that the class of houses proposed the following year, and eventually completed as nos. 3 to 8, by Robert Edwards appears to have been accepted only with reluctance[213]. The most substantial agreement on this earlier, eastern side was with Philip Meldrum, who was also responsible for much building in the southern part of St Thomas's road, now disappeared under the Kingshold estate. Leases to Meldrum and his assignees (nos.9 to 20) were granted variously between 1866 and 1868[214]. (The west side, Poole's charity land, is considered below.)

In January of 1867, the Cass trustees resolved to drive forward the process of developing the rest of the estate, and to invite tenders for the remainder of the undeveloped land[215]. Cassland road, together with Bradstock (formerly Union) road and Bramshaw (formerly Brampton) roads, was gradually built up throughout the ensuing ten years, the latter beginning with no. 6, "Heartley House", in 1867, for Robert Lishman, who then financed George Beckett to build nos. 8 and 10.

The earliest 19th century development on Cassland road had been on the north and eastern part, in the late 1850's: and this had been followed in 1862/3 by a long terrace built by George Catling, on the site now occupied by the school building. Later there were two main spurts of development on these two side roads, in 1866/8 and 1874/5, the first perhaps given its impetus by increased activity south of the road on Wright's building land. Along Cassland road itself building continued steadily, and in small parcels, until 1881. An exactly parallel pattern was followed on Bentham road (which formerly extended some distance further to the east), including the now-demolished northern side[216].

Nos. 4-28 Bentham road having been constructed by City builders sub-contracting (in exactly what way is not clear) from the Innes brothers, in the two years following their building agreement of 1860, such part of the remaining agreement land as was not developed at that time (nos 30 to 42, together with 25 to 31 Bradstock road) resulted from their sub-contracting to John Scholtes, one of Bagge's builders on the Norris estate, who completed the terrace between 1872 and 1875.

The Poole estate and Cassland crescent

Perhaps inspired by this increased attention to the northern boundary, the parish authorities, as trustees of Poole's charity, turned their attention about this time to building, having in 1865 recovered their land at the termination of a 7 year lease for pasture, to Williams, cowkeeper, of Well street. (This, when entered into in the doldrums of 1858, had been far from a preliminary to intended building activity; the lessee had been required to lay down 12 loads per acre of "good rotten dung" every three years[217].) When they did see the opportunity of building, they had the good sense to employ an old Hackney hand as their surveyor and negotiator. George Wales, better than anyone, was able to do a sensible deal on the realignment of boundaries with the Cass estate. It was he who, acting for the building developer, after a proposal to build the eastern half of Cassland crescent as a mirror-image of the western had been accepted, proposed that the remaining houses in the crescent be given an extra storey: his successor as Cass estate surveyor could only report, mildly, that there was no objection unless uniformity was sought. No objection was found[218].

In May 1865, the parish authorities entered into a building contract with G. J. Bishop, who early in the following year took leases of the houses he had built in Valentine, Poole and Terrace roads, and on the northern arm of Queen Anne road, as it was then conceived, facing the Redgrave properties on Kenton road which fronted George Oldfield's ropeworks. Bishop's building continued throughout the rest of the decade, completing Cassland crescent (with the houses, now nos. 25 to 39, he called Cedar and Crescent villas) and "Bishop's road" by 1870. Like many another developer seeking immortality, his misfortune was to commemorate himself by a street name too frequently used: his verbal memorial was to find itself obscured in 1907 by the conversion of Bishop's road to the honouring of the most distinguished of South Hackney's many notable M.P.'s, Charles Russell, later Lord Russell of Killowen.

Bishop's work for Poole's charity was complete by 1874, with 234-8 Well street and the remaining parts of Queen Anne road [219].

The final phase

The remaining years of the 1860's saw what was left of building land filling up fast, with the completion of the roads branching from Cassland road and round what came to be called the Broadway (Lauriston road).

The Cass trustees may well have been reserving the area to the south and east of Hackney terrace, known from the grazing tenant as "Tyler's Field", as a possible site for the relocation of the Aldgate schoolhouse. By 1868, when the decision had been taken to rebuild in Aldgate, the residents of the terrace saw, in a very nearly literal sense, the writing on the wall. Word went round that the gates at the bottom of their gardens were to be bricked up; the inference was all too clearly that the communal pleasure ground was to become building land. Accordingly a petition went to the trustees protesting against such an idea: the founder of the charity, they pleaded, touchingly if misguidedly, had intended the Lawn for their recreation[220].

But the rumour was all too accurate; very shortly afterwards the trustees commissioned a survey of the development potential of their remaining land, of which Hackney terrace lawn, with its possibility of a frontage onto the Common, could only be a prime example. Nevertheless, the protest had its effect, or at any rate could be accommodated for the time being. Only "Tyler's field", that is to say largely the site of Meynell road and the adjacent Cassland road frontage (so called after the tenant-farmer of the 1850's) and half of the area to the east of the lawn, used as a playground for the boys of Grove house school, were appropriated for building at this stage - due as much to lack of market interest as to tenant protest. The only short-term effect on the terrace was the decision, in October 1869, to curtail what must at all events have seemed the extraordinarily large garden at no. 18[221].

In subsequent lettings of the terrace, care was taken to ensure that rights over the lawn did not form part of the lease - instead, a separate subscription of £1 per year was asked. The rules for its management were revised in 1878, and the restriction on smoking rescinded altogether. The gate from the Common was to be locked at 6 in winter and 8 in summer; and tenants were expressly requested to ensure that it was closed after daytime use, "that horses and cattle might not enter from the Common". Urbanisation had yet its limits[222].

This tension between the residual rural character of the neighbourhood and its inexorable conversion into a suburb also took other forms. For long the criss-crossing of paths across the Common had been a source of friction between the estate owners and their tenants, and had led to its abandonment for arable crops; an early signal of trouble was the fair held to celebrate peace in the Crimea in June 1856. Even the grazing tenant found it an irritant when local inhabitants used the field for pitching cricket tents in the summer. The eventual substitution of recreational for agricultural uses, following the Metropolitan Commons Acts of 1866 onwards, seems to have been compensated for somewhat by the use of the grass in Cassland crescent for grazing, perhaps in response to tenants' complaints that it was overgrown and unkempt. But despite their search for ever more building land, the trustees had the sense to reject a proposal to build small houses on the "Kenton road triangle"[223].

The surviving segment of Gascoyne road, overlooking the Common, was built up by the two Samuels Tucker, of Queen Anne road, in 1870. Occupation of Meynell road, let under a building agreement to the Goodman brothers, began in 1877 (after a request from them for an extension, or a peppercorn rent, rather than being held to their original, pre-dated agreement). When begun, however, development (together with the associated building of 56-90 Cassland road) proved one of the most successful letting propositions the estate had ever witnessed, being completed and for the most part let to investors or occupiers by the autumn of 1879, although despite the landlord's earlier forbearance the developers denied liability under the agreement for making up the roads[224].

The north-eastern Cass estate: a sample of the pattern of building agreements

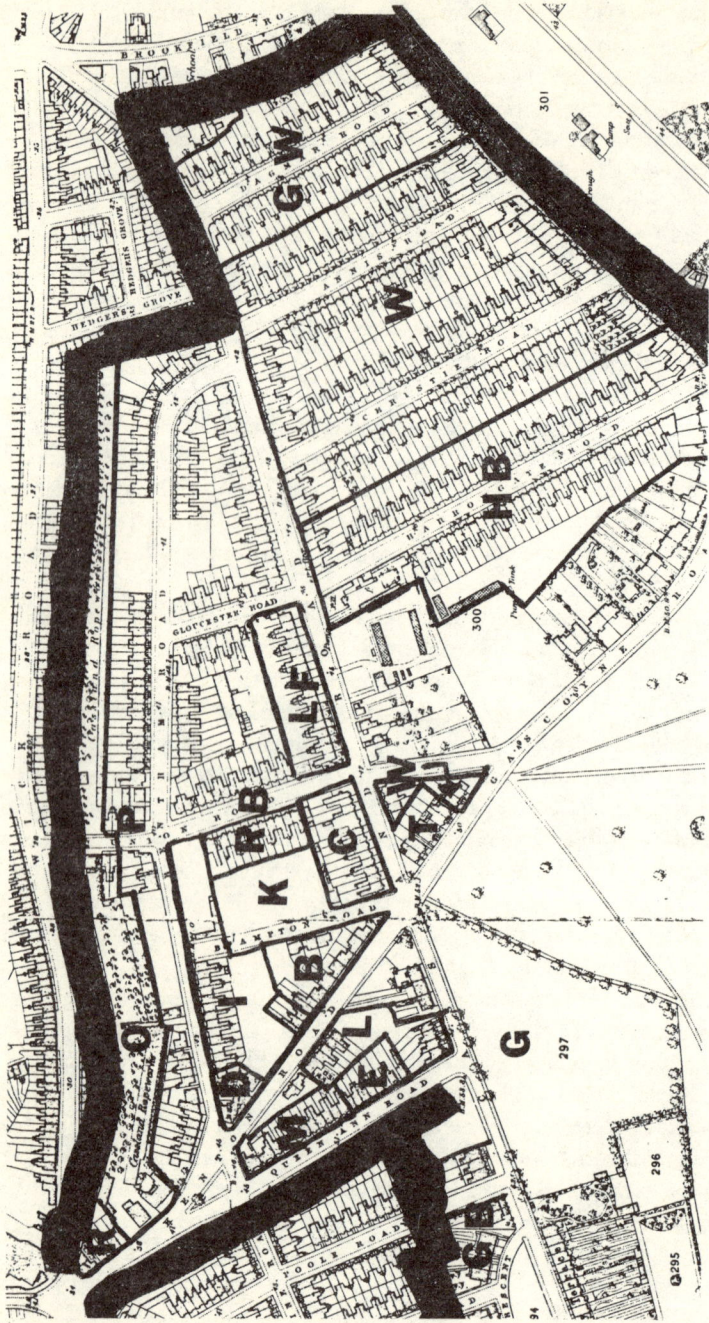

Names in brackets are those of principal sub-contractors

B: Beckett. GB: Bishop. HB: Bagge. RB: Banks. C: Catling. D: Day. E: Edwards. GW: Glaskin (Wright). G: Goodman. I: Innes. K: Kelly. L: Lewis. LF: Lefever. M: Meldrum. O: Oldfield. P: Phillips. R: Redgrave. T: Tucker. W: Wright.

Completion of the development of this portion of the estate could not be long delayed in such circumstances, not least because by 1879 lines for horse-drawn trams from the Docks came along Cassland road. It was early recognised that a sensible building line at the rear of the terrace would necessitate an exchange of land with the parish authorities administering South's charity on the Common; but it was not until 1892 that the tenant of 18 Hackney terrace was notified that still more of his garden would be required[225].

Between July 1891 and February 1892 the brothers Charles and Henry Winkley built Queen's Gate villas, securing 90 year leases, on the strip of land squeezed between the Common and Victoria park road, west of a villa ("Brampton cottage") built for his own occupation by the builder George Catling in 1855. After some further hard bargaining, and what was for a South Hackney estate an unusually competitive course of dealing, they also took a building lease of what was to become Meynell crescent; virtually all the leases granted between the first, in September 1893, and the last, in May 1895, were swiftly assigned or sublet, frequently to existing residents of South Hackney - the King Edward's road phenomenon all over again. The Winkleys renewed the tradition of partial owner-occupation.

As the century ended, the only remaining development land was on the sites of the large houses of the 1780's - Common (Grove) house, Terrace lodge and Grove cottage, latterly called "the Limes". In the 1890's this latter became a club, the house being let from year to year and in constant need of repair and improvement. In 1900 the land was acquired for building by Arthur Barsht, who renewed another tradition by building eleven houses on a site originally intended for ten; "Limes terrace" and the neighbouring houses on the north west corner of Terrace road, were the result. The site of the estate surveyor's house was eventually absorbed into the college site established to the west[226].

The remaining 18th century properties, apart from the enduring Hackney terrace, survived until the 1930's, when Common (Grove) house (latterly a deaconesses' home) and Terrace lodge were bought by Classic Estates Ltd., a private company established by the Morris and Sheinman families, whose first venture had been a three-storey development on the corner of Mare street and Morning lane. Blenheim cottages were, at the expiry of the Clark lease, again divorced from their back land, and Meynell gardens (nicknamed "Little Hampstead" by the company, with subsequent support from Pevsner) was the result. Further developments followed: Sharon Gardens, an infill of rear gardens in Victoria Park road, and Classic mansions in Shore road, behind Well street[227].

Completing the Crown estate

It has already been noted that there was no activity on the Crown's building land in South Hackney in the 1850's, although the division of plots and layout of streets had been drawn up by Pennethorne in 1854; and indeed building did not begin in earnest on the Old Ford side of the Park until 1858, after which time it continued steadily through the 1860's, beginning in Old Ford road and reaching Approach road in 1862[228].

The building land had from the outset been set aside from the Park itself, being fenced and let partly for grazing, or, as in the case of one and a quarter acres on the north of Grove street lane, for leisure gardening by local residents. Increased activity by builders plainly alarmed the 18 gardeners here, as in 1859 they petitioned the Commissioners of Woods and Forests to be allowed to retain their plots until they were imminently required for building. "We have hitherto grown potatoes and other vegetables very useful for the maintenance of our families", they explained, continuing with an appeal to social policy: "its cultivation has been of great benefit to all of us, withdrawing many from public houses and inducing generally habits of sobriety and providence"[229].

Their adherence to such Victorian values was to be safe for a few more years, as when building began in South Hackney it was in Victoria Park road, and even then it began in a gradual fashion. The first lease was in 1860, to Garrett Nagle, a Bethnal Green builder, formerly a contractor on the very different Bradshaw development of 1845, nearby; in the same year R. E. Borton set out on several years' development of the Crown and neighbouring Cass property on the south side of Victoria Park road, beginning next to the Sir John Cass pub and working eastwards until, in 1863, he completed the Royal Standard[230].

All the Crown leases, whenever granted, were drawn so as to fall in in 1954, so Borton began with a term of 92 years, reduced in later leases. Borton seems to have been responsible for much of the Crown building in Victoria Park road, although he for one used an architect, Joseph Harris, for the pub as well as his double-fronted villas. The houses on the south side of the road are notable in South Hackney for the quantity of stabling provided - notable, that is, at any time, let alone at this relatively late date. The surviving villas are notably similar to Hugh Eastman's group opposite; Borton's earliest building was so contemporary with Eastman's that it is now impossible to judge safely which came first[231].

Much of Borton's frontage has gone, as has Henry Bagge's contribution of four large villas facing the Park, apparently to his own design; and the house which became the family home of the Booths of the Salvation Army, no. 3 Gore road. Part of Thomas Ennor's St Agnes terrace of 1863, however, survives, by the Park's main northern entrance. (Ennor was also responsible for the Bedford Hotel, on Thomas

Natt's land, developed in 1868-9 a decade after Natt's death.)[232]

In 1864 building started on the triangular building plot at Wick lane, where all that is left of this development is Cadogan terrace, the Hackney portion of which was built in 1869/70, principally by the Hackney Wick builder H. R. Allen. Other building was financed at least in part by J. C. Baum, landlord of the White Lion, whose other building in the curtilage of his tavern included cottages opposite the Park which he named Deerfoot cottages, in pleasing commemoration of a race run on his running ground by the American Indian athlete[233].

In 1867 another Borton, Alfred, established a building frontage along the south side of Grove street lane; originally undertaking to build 16 semi-detached villas, he was permitted, instead, to put up 26 smaller houses. Once again the South Hackney land market had failed to meet the landowner's aspirations[234].

South Hackney was by this time a very densely developed area, a fact recognised by the Commissioners themselves in fulfilling their long-standing intention of releasing building land for a church, St Augustine's, built in the eastern part of the park south of Brookfield road, in 1867. The original thinking about church building seems to have assumed that the church would be designed to serve the residents of Park property, but St Augustine's, at 1000 seats, went far beyond any such requirement.

In 1871 the Commissioners' agreement with Joseph Lucas for building leases close to Alfred Borton's houses on Grove street lane, on one of six plots remaining of the Park building land, seems to have stimulated a Parliamentary question as to the estimated value of the remaining land. Behind the question lay considerable concern from local residents, and notably those of Borton's earlier development, as to the Commissioners' intentions and the potential effect of further building on the amenity of the Park[235].

This was not a new theme. As early as 1856 there had been comment in the press on the undesirability of allocating Park land for "a horrid building scheme". In November 1871 a meeting of the Victoria Park Preservation Society, which appears to have been called into being to "consider the best means of arresting further building development on the Crown lands surrounding Victoria Park", took place at the Town hall, chaired by George Dornbusch. The Medical Officer of Health, Dr Tripe, reported on the swollen population of South Hackney, which had nearly quadrupled since 1851. A press campaign followed, the allegations made being regarded in government quarters with a mixture of indignation, resignation and cynicism - the part of the park in alleged jeopardy not being at the time, or for that matter hitherto, used by the public, as claimed, but "by cows, bullocks and horses. The piece opposite Mr Dornbusch's house is used by about 20 bullocks at this very time. Someone ought to write to the Standard"[236].

Officials noted with distaste that Plummer, one of the three prime movers of the campaign "used to be something of a correspondent to newspapers, I think what is known as a 'penny-a-liner'". One fact was clear, however: in 1853 Pennethorne had estimated the revenue from house-building at a little over £6097; by November 1871 it stood at some £2450.

The public campaign proved powerful enough to secure an interview with the Chancellor of the Exchequer, Robert Lowe, who was reported as saying that he would do what he could to assist the inhabitants to purchase the remaining land themselves, so long as any public money was found from local rates, not national taxes. In any event the Crown Commissioners were reluctant to back down on negotiations they had already got to an advanced stage; moreover they considered the unbuilt land to the north west of the Park unsuitable for adding to the recreational area, as being separated from the main corpus of the Park by a public road. This left some 29 acres open to negotiation. The Metropolitan Board of Works put in their offer, in January 1872, for some 24 acres of this total, and these changed hands for some £20,450, based on £85 per acre at 16 years' purchase, the agreement being formalised by Act of Parliament. Thus the stretch south of Grove street lane, so far as unbuilt on or already agreed for, was secured for the public. "The Chancellor...has turned the transaction to good account, and has managed to get rid of the least valuable part of the thirty acres", commented the Hackney Express[237].

By 1874, the building land left unallocated consisted of a plot on the east side of St Thomas's (Skipworth) road, built up from 1875 onwards; and land set aside at the extreme east of the Park and elsewhere for a church and for "parsonages". The Victoria Park Preservation Society was unable to interest the Metropolitan Board in securing any more of this land, although the Board subsequently took on the management of the Park.

Although negotiations for new agreements were aborted, Lucas had proceeded with the building that had sparked the campaign, which resulted in Cawley and Rockmead roads, now demolished, all of which let readily in 1873/4, no doubt the more so because of the frontage to the Park. W. B. Dyer and Mark Bean, both of whom had previously been involved with building agreements near Victoria Park road on the Cass estate, also participated in this development and in Gore road. Gore road leases dated from 1872, those in the Crescent part not until 1875, building continuing here until 1879. Time after time the same financiers crop up: S. Barnett, Thomas Greenwood (an oil dealer, from Lauriston road Broadway), W. J. Avenell, Thomas Beven. The impression is very much that South Hackney residents and existing investors were by this time confidently backing local development. The final stage of the Crown estate building justified their confidence.

Part Four: Living in South Hackney

The residents

W.S. Clarke, writing a handbook for discerning London householders of 1881 who were in search of a comfortable and economical residence, was at pains to assure southern and western sceptics of the merits of Hackney. Although round the Downs, he wrote, the handsome houses may still be the residences of those "opulent and respectable" inhabitants for which the district was once remarkable -

"the old Annine and Georgian houses of the main street, with their relics of pleasure grounds, gardens and stabling, are not as a rule tenanted by the eminent merchants, bankers and wealthy retired tradesfolk such as those whose horses and carriages were to be seen standing before the doors of obsequious shopkeepers even as lately as thirty years ago. It happens therefore that a number of large, convenient and substantial houses are let at sums ranging from £70 to £120 a year, chiefly, however, because of the ample grounds formerly attached to them having been included in the building leases for smaller adjacent houses. Starting from Cambridge Heath, there are a few houses of this description before reaching what is properly the high street of Hackney; and on the right, reached by Victoria Park road and King Edward's road is the extensive district of South Hackney, adjoining Victoria Park, and consisting of some large and handsome houses from £75 to £100 a year; a large area of smaller but still convenient villas from £45 to £75; and smaller residences, inhabited by a large number of employes and others engaged in the City, at rents below £45."

This is indicative not only of Clarke's intended readership but of the relative status of the Norris estate, where in 1890 the average annual rental was assessed to be £35. In 1869, the local house agent on the Norris estate was advertising houses at £270-£700 purchase, and £27 to £60 rental[238].

Clarke went on to comment that the water supply, from the Lea filter beds of the East London waterworks, "has greatly improved during the past few years", and that gas was supplied by the Imperial Gas Company. Mains sewerage had in fact arrived in 1860, the works to create the high level intercepting sewer creating havoc on Well street common and causing subsidence at the western end of Cassland crescent[239].

In modern times residence in South Hackney has always been dominated by the area's relationship with the City. From the time at which the Norris and Cass families, like others to the north, established their country houses here, the principal focus of the residents' employment and the source of their wealth has been the business district, little more than a mile off via Shoreditch and the Hackney road, where residents employed other than in services supporting the other members of the community either exercised their business or profession or sold the produce of their land.

The City was always readily accessible, on a daily basis, on foot or horseback. Families such as the wealthy Norrises also maintained a City home; City shopkeepers, such as the Ryder family, resident in Urswick road in the early 18th century, divided their time between their City premises and their Hackney home. By the time Hackney terrace was built, it is probable that few if any of its residents had another home, travelling in to town daily if their business took them there. The occupations of the very earliest residents of the terrace - other than the developer, the attorney Thomas Abree Pickering, and the Unitarian minister Robert Aspland - are now not known with certainty, although they are unlikely to differ greatly from those represented in the parish census of 1811, which reveals City merchants and brokers, "gentlemen" with no occupation, a stationer from Covent Garden, and two (probably naval) "Captains"[240].

Thus was the pattern set which was consolidated in the 1860's and obtains up to the present time. The earliest Victorian terraces and villas which grew up around Hackney terrace and near the Park attracted well-to-do merchants and people of independent means; such were the populations of Victoria park road and Cassland crescent. In place of the most fastidious residents of Hackney terrace, who deserted the tall narrow Georgian houses for the St Thomas's estate, while there remained a proportion of families with direct commercial interests, came the ubiquitous clerk. Inevitably this portmanteau description fits not only senior bank officials but more humble pen-pushers, and Victorian South Hackney from King Edward's road to Dagmar road came to be peopled with clerks whose precise place in their respective hierarchies cannot be known, even though occasionally identified as a notary's, a "commercial", or a railway clerk; and can only be assumed from the size and style of the houses in which they chose, or could afford, to live.

If the Hackney terrace Captains of 1811 were indeed sailors, they exemplify another persistent strand in the composition of South Hackney society: marine trades have been, to a degree which is today surprising for an area 2 miles from the river, steadily represented from the time at which occupations are ascertainable - certainly well before the development of direct public transport routes to the riverside. The presence of such as Customs officers, ropemakers and seafarers' families demonstrates that the City was not the sole focus of the area's economy. Indeed, by 1869, Well street contained three separate establishments selling marine stores. In St Thomas's churchyard, by Mare street, is a poignant memorial to the young son of a local family, who in 1822 "fell from the masthead and was killed".

Industrial employment was available locally from an early date, replacing horticulture as important local employment as market gardens were built over. The Berger paintworks were established in Homerton in 1773; by the middle of the next century the factory chimneys of the much-expanded business dominated the view northwards along Well street. The Cassland ropeworks arrived in 1848, more land-than labour-intensive, with a payroll of 60; the parish also housed workers at the Xylonite/Parkesine works in Homerton in the 1860's, and at the dye works at Hackney Wick.

Most of the larger houses, throughout the period, were staffed by at least one resident female servant; two or three are occasionally found in Hackney terrace or King Edward's road, particularly where the family contained young children. In Annis or Christie roads, whose typical population consisted of clerks and skilled tradesmen, 42 out of 113 households in 1871 had one resident servant. The female residents of the area typically exceeded the male by a ratio of upwards of 5:4, a ratio which changed relatively little between 1841 and 1871, a period during which the population of the area, some 3,500 in 1841, grew fourfold.

For the years for which census information is available, there is relatively small incidence of multi-occupation of houses. It occurred as much by sub-division or boarding in an occasional large villa on Victoria Park road as in the smaller streets, and was commonplace on the Freehold Land Society development in its earliest years. In Annis/Christie in 1871 there were only 2 houses shared by more than one family, and 14 taking in boarders not part of the family.

If there were extremes of wealth and poverty, neither was on an extensive scale. In 1834, only four residents of South Hackney, (H.H. Norris, Dr Algernon Frampton and two residents of Shore place) were owners of sufficient property to hold the Parliamentary franchise[241]. After development, the area never attracted the very wealthiest, although many of those it did attract were wealthy enough to speculate in property development on a small scale.

Poverty was never unknown; at the beginning of the 18th century residents of Grove street and Water gruel row were poor enough to be excused rates year after year, or to choose to discharge their civic liability for highway maintenance by offering labour in lieu of payment. At the close of the 19th century Charles Booth's researchers observed, of the district bounded by Mare street, Well street, Lauriston road and the Park: "The main roads...contain a good class of shopkeepers and professional men, whose houses are fairly large, with decent gardens. A certain amount of distress in some of the smaller places, mainly caused by poor and irregular work."

Of the eastern half of the parish, extending to North street and the canal, there were found to be "many well to do people, with a large sprinkling of comfortable artisans and clerks. A few poor people in the southern end, casual labourers whose wives sometime work out." In other words, poverty was concentrated in Bradshaw's development, to the rear of Gore road, and around the Prior's house in Well street, as well as in the neighbourhood of the Wick and in North (Northiam) street. In a population just short of 13,000, some 2,000 fulfilled Booth's criterion of poor as opposed to "comfortable" circumstances, of whom only 212 were in extreme distress, all of these in the eastern part of the area[242].

Booth's maps, which make his analysis vivid, identify very subtle distinctions in South Hackney social strata at the end of the 19th century. Whereas Hackney is devoid of any residents described as "Upper Middle and Upper Classes, wealthy" (the nearest area so delineated being Highbury New Park), all of Victoria Park road, east and west; King Edward's road; Cassland road; Gascoyne and Meynell roads and the eastern portion of the Norris estate qualify as "Well-to-do, middle class".

Here are some refinements of extreme niceness. Southborough road (west side), Warneford and Fremont streets, Shore road and Tudor road as well as the remainder of the Cass estate and Crown estate are regarded as "Fairly comfortable. Good ordinary earnings"; whereas only a handful of terraces fall below this level. The rubric "Mixed. Some comfortable, others poor" distinguishes the perception (borne out in census data) that the Lauriston road frontage was noticeably less affluent than the rest of the Norris estate, and comparable with one street on the Frampton estate, east of Frampton park road, as well as Wick road, Hedger's grove and Silk Mill row.

Only Homer road, Percy road, Morpeth road and Providence row were "Poor", earning 18s. to 21s. a week "for a moderate family". "Very poor, chronic want" was confined to Victoria grove on Bradshaw's estate as well as Palace road and the immediate neighbourhood of this easternmost of the Frampton streets, and a courtyard on the south west corner of Well street. The closest of Booth's notorious dark purple patches ("Lowest class. Vicious, semi-criminal") were in Chapman road at the Wick and, more prominently, in Homerton.

Estate control

Some residents, of course, carried on business from home; on the large estates this would be in direct conflict with covenants in the lease, which prohibited use of the premises for business or alteration of their appearance, and, in their most developed form, use other than as a private dwelling. The Cass estate responded firmly to pressure from other residents to enforce their rights as landlords, insisting that a bootmaker in Harrowgate road desist from hanging boots outside his house by way of advertisement, and that a resident in Meynell road refrain from displaying a window blind advertising his business. Residents on the smaller estates had no such effective constraint, whatever their neighbours may have felt, and even Cass residents in Brampton and Kenton roads could achieve little once a lease for a mason's yard had been granted. The developed form of lease on the Cass estate even enabled the trustees to prevent a house being used as "a receptacle for lunatics"[243].

The Cass estate however, where the surveyor could find no objection to a tenant's proposition for a non-permitted use, readily agreed to it: thus for example a business manufacturing Valentine cards was set up near the eastern border of the estate, and

Cassland road frontages converted into shops. Often the surveyor would be given discretion to permit alterations to premises if affected neighbours could see no objection.

St Thomas's policy was either deliberately liberal, or simply lax. Their early leases afforded them almost, if not quite, as much control as the contemporary Cass leases: no effective objection could be taken to Glaskin subdividing his premises at 26 Shore road, any more than to Robert Kitteridge's third house on his plot for two in Kenton road. Instead of a covenant restraining use other than as a private dwelling, however, as was evolved through the experience of the other estates, there was a short shopping-list of prohibitions: shop, public house, steam engine, building yard or workshop, for which the landowner's consent was required; and there remained no such restriction on new building. These prohibitions could have been enough, had the will been there, to prevent the character of the Well street frontage of their property changing; if the will was there, any attempt must have been futile. 1884 saw the arrival of Henry Sharman's wholesale bootmaking business, in William Norris's property at no. 74; another business, Preston's, being established on the north side about the same time. Within a decade Well street had become the home of 17 different leatherworking factories and their attendant suppliers, leaving aside the retail end of the business in evidence elsewhere nearby, all of them established in the spacious terraced property between 58 and 74 Well street, or in the smaller Norris property at 40-46, or on the blocks on the north side exactly opposite these stretches. The somewhat unimaginative covenants might not have been able to prevent the wholesale suppliers moving in, but without the workshops, in practice little different from full-scale factories, which could have been prevented, the pressure for warehouse conversion would never have been present.

The subsequent history of this northern segment of the St Thomas's estate is thereafter one of the gradual encroachment of other light industries; and particularly the shoemaking industry, so that Well street became, with London Fields, one of London's most concentrated areas of this activity by 1901. By the time when in the 1920's a process of negotiating surrender and renewal of the various St Thomas's leases was begun, not only this segment of Well street but also much of the eastern part of St Thomas's estate to the north of King Edward's road had ceased to be residential at all[244].

How far these developments can be attributed to lack of pressure from local residents, and how far to the greater size and greater remoteness from them of St Thomas's estate management, can at this distance only be a subject for speculation.

Transport

Before the late 1830's, the traveller Citywards who did not have his own horse transport was compelled to walk or make use of the so-called short stage coaches which served the areas surrounding the capital beyond the central area where hackney cabs had a monopoly.

The traveller in other directions was not so well served. Robert Aspland, Minister at the Gravel Pit chapel in Chatham place, was in 1805, during his residence in Hackney terrace, invited by the congregation at the sister chapel at Newington Green to minister to them also. He declined, on the chief ground that "the distance....from Hackney terrace...and the want of all publick stages on the road, I have all along considered as a serious objection..." It was estimated, however, about his time that there were about 40 to 50 hackney carriages available for hire within the parish[245].

A few premises, such as Hackney terrace, had their own stabling, although it seems improbable that all the residents there provided themselves with mounts. Later, only the Crown estate villas on the south side of Victoria park road were comparably provided for; elsewhere commercial coach housing or stabling was built, as on the northern stretch of Lauriston road, attached to shopkeepers' premises, or by T. F. Kelly behind the Alexandra pub.

When the horse buses arrived the hire trade was destroyed. By 1843 at least two operators were providing services through South Hackney to the City and the West End; bookings could be taken in Well street. Indeed many more services will have been available nearby, as by 1859 there were daily some 390 bus journeys each way between Shoreditch church and Cambridge Heath. Until tolls were abolished in 1864, carriages might pay a toll of between fourpence and ninepence, depending on the number of horses, at the Cambridge Heath or Mile End Gate turnpikes, or any of the numerous side-gates at which the turnpike system was entered; a single horse was charged at a penny in winter, a penny-halfpenny in summer. The buses as distinct from their horsepower seem to have been exempt from tolls, not having been contemplated when the turnpike legislation was examined by Parliament in 1826[246].

The coming of larger volume transport coincided approximately with the time at which the development potential of the area could be realised by the major landowners, with the falling in of the long 18th century leases; and with the inception of the Park. Central Hackney had its own railway station when the North London railway was opened in 1850; South Hackney was served from 1856 by the so-called Victoria Park station, and accessible via the Homerton station after 1868. It was not until 1865 however that the line ran directly into the City at Broad street; before that time the journey was more circuitous, to Fenchurch street via Bow[247].

A strip of land behind Eastman's villas on Victoria park road, which he was licensed to let to a trimmings manufacturer, came into the possession of George Wales in 1864 after he had left the employment of the Cass estate, and became established as a cab rank, to the distress of local residents. That there was a need for more commercial cabs was evident from the comments of the French Hospital committee, who had complained of the difficulty of travelling from town to Victoria Park road some three years earlier[248].

By 1879 horse trams extended to Hackney Wick through Lauriston road to the western end of Cassland road, on the still-extant bus route to the docks; many more services were available on Mare street, on the routes between Hackney, Clapton, the City and the West End[249].

Shopping

When Hackney terrace was built, residents looked beyond South Hackney for most of their supplies. There were cow-keepers at Heart Place (west of Kenton road) and Grove street. Butter and cheese and other groceries would be obtained from shops in Church street and shoes from the Hackney road. Even though other goods might be available in Hackney, someone working in the City might find it more convenient to shop there (as surviving household bills suggest) for candles perhaps[250].

Goods became available more readily locally with the early 19th century development of the northern section of Well street. By 1869 it was the main shopping street, with shops and small businesses along its full length, but concentrated most heavily at two points: near the junction with Mare street, and north of the junction with Cassland road. Taking Terrace road and Valentine road as essentially part of the same shopping area, Well street had 8 grocers, 8 shops selling drapery and textiles, 7 bakeries, 6 each of beershops, butchers and bootmakers, 4 chemists, 5 greengrocers, 4 oil and paint shops, 4 tailors, 3 each of cheesemongers, furniture shops, fishmongers and marine stores, and two each of corn dealers, hairdressers, haberdashers and china and glass merchants. There were also more than twenty other specialised businesses, selling things like music, baby linen, tea, tin or ironmongery, or services such as plumbing, gasfitting and mending carts and carriages. The exhausted shopper had a choice of 4 coffee houses or dining rooms and an eel pie shop at which to take refreshment.

On a much smaller scale, initially, was the shopping round the junction between Victoria Park road and the Broadway (Lauriston road, south of the roundabout). Here could be found, in 1869, the full range of food shops, plus a bootmaker, an undertaker, a draper, a brushmaker, two general shops, two tobacconists, two "fancy repositories"

Well street, looking south down Mare street, in the 1870's

and a "bazaar". With the building of Alexandra terrace (130-160 Victoria park road, 1870/1) other shops and small businesses arrived.

In Kenton road, Cassland road and Palace road - on sites now largely redeveloped - were small groups of shops of the "corner shop" kind, supplying mostly food, tobacco and supplies for heating and lighting.

Schools and institutions

South Hackney was never short of schools. In the 17th century the Hackney district as a whole was famed for its schools, and children were sent there from the City. Robert Ainsworth, who leased the Norris family house before its rebuilding in 1729, and after whom Ainsworth road is named, inherited and consolidated this tradition. Many of these schools were transient indeed. Dame schools abounded; academies for young ladies and young gentlemen sprang up and passed away, notably around Tryon's place and Mare street. Among them was the French Academy, run in partnership by the Swiss, Paul de la Pierre, sometime tenant of John Wowen's estate[251]. In 1821 there were eight different schools in South Hackney alone. Considerably later, two neighbouring houses in Hackney terrace housed for a time a girls' school and a boys' school, run by a sister and brother respectively; Ainsworth road had a college for young gentlemen. Just beyond the parish was Wick Hall school, an establishment with some pretensions if its prospectus of 1841 is any guide.

Two of the longest lived boys' boarding schools were in Grove street. The first was run by R. S. Barnes, in the old Cass house or a house on its site, his predecessor there, James Pickbourne, also having been a schoolmaster. This was known as Grove house school, and at its height catered for upwards of 40 pupils. In the 1840's its successor emerged in the school run by John Willey at "Common house", the Riddle house facing Well street common. When Grove house school closed and the house became the home of the Offor family, the former Cass house continued to be known as Grove house but the name Grove house school was adopted, no doubt gratefully, by the younger establishment.

For the poorer parishioners schooling was provided only by non-conformist interests - the Village Itineracy, of the Well street chapel - before 1834, when Henry Handley Norris, as befitted his role as co-founder of the National Society for Promoting the Education of the Poor in the Principles of the Established Church, endowed the South Hackney Charity School, established east of the path from Grove street to Cassland road[252].

These buildings had to be removed when the new church came to be built, and after a spell in buildings later taken over by the Theological college the school was removed to a larger site in Greenwood's row, given by St Thomas's Hospital, where the new buildings were designed by the Hospital's surveyor, Henry Currey.

In exchange for the site of the old school the trustees obtained from the church building Commissioners a site opposite Monger's almshouses, which they leased to the builder Samuel Abell who had constructed houses called Park place on the adjoining plot to the west. In 1853 he built and was granted a lease of Bellevue Cottages, the

Grove House School, South Hackney near London

Grove (Common) house school, looking north west from Well street common income forming an endowment for the school trust[253].

South Hackney has also played host to institutions whose work had wider frontiers. The oldest-established of these was the British Penitent Female Refuge, which involved itself in rescue work among women forced into prostitution and crime. Founded in Bethnal Green in 1829, it subsequently moved to Cambridge Heath; subsequently the Elizabeth Fry Refuge for released prisoners took over the early 18th century house at 195 Mare Street.

The Theological college buildings in Well street were themselves subsequently acquired by the Bethnal green parish authorities to supplement their workhouse accommodation. No. 26 King Edward's road became, about 1900, the Ayahs' home, offering accommodation to women from the Indian sub-continent who had come to this country in the role of nursemaid to the children of British families.

Religious and Social life

At the beginning of the 19th century there were three places of worship in the South Hackney division of Hackney parish. The chapel of ease, built in 1809 by subscription from the Norris, Frampton, de Kewer and Powell families among others, was a small but impressive classical building situated at the foot of St Thomas's place. By the 1840's, with systematic development about to start in the area, it was already too small. A plan was launched to replace it on St Thomas's land near Shore place, but was abandoned, perhaps because more suitable land became available on the Currie estate. Eventually mission rooms appeared on the old chapel site, in the 1880's housing the South Hackney soup kitchen[254].

The other chapels in the early 19th century were that of the so-called Village Itineracy, at the western point of Cassland road, to which the Theological college was later attached; and another dissenting chapel was built in 1810 in Shore place, under an agreement of 1810 with the Hospital. This was pulled down when the area was set aside for building in the mid-1840's[255]. A congregation which had formerly met on the site of 2 Shore road formed the nucleus of the Mare street Baptist chapel, built in 1811.

The new parish church, dedicated to St John of Jerusalem in the light of the association of South Hackney with the Order, was designed, by E. C. Hakewill, to seat 1,000, and consecrated in 1848. Even this was not sufficient some fifteen years later, when the same architect was commissioned to design St Augustine's, of similar size, within the Park itself, on a site now marked only by a quadrangle of plane trees; in 1870 there came the smaller Christ Church, in Gore road[256].

The Hampden chapel of 1847 is almost exactly contemporary with the parish church; it was built as a daughter church to the Mare street Baptist Chapel. Other non-conformist premises were the Presbyterian hall in St Thomas's road (23-7

The Well street (Village Itineracy) chapel, on the corner of Cassland road

Ainsworth road), more recently a synagogue; and two methodist establishments, the Tyndale Primitive Methodist Memorial Chapel in Brookfield road, constructed about 1890, and the earlier methodist chapel on the north side of Cassland road, replaced after substantial bomb damage by Stuart House.

A congregational chapel was built in 1865 at Cambridge Heath, replacing an earlier iron church on land bought from Marmaduke Matthews in the grounds of his villa: an example of the infilling noted by W. S. Clarke. The bells chased William and Catherine Booth from their home in Cambridge lodge villas to the relative seclusion of 3 Gore road. The Trinity chapel in Lauriston road, built on the former site of a box factory and a confectioner's premises, belongs to the early years of this century[257].

The St Thomas's square chapel, home to a very long-standing Presbyterian congregation, stood on the east side of Mare street south of St Thomas's square. Its burial ground deteriorated in the latter 19th century into an unofficial garbage dump known, before being taken in hand by the municipal open spaces committee, as "the dust hole"[258].

Much social life that was not centred on the church must have centred on the pubs, with which the area was - relative to the rest of Hackney, if not necessarily to the rest of East London - tolerably well provided. It was always so; in 1843 South Hackney contained several pubs, from the old Three Colts and the Swiss Cottage (on the site of Abbeyfield house) in Grove street to the Green Dragon and Two Black Boys in Well street, the latter just beyond the boundary, as were the Rose and Crown at Cambridge Heath and the White Lion at the Wick. Mare street offered the Flying Horse opposite the end of Well street, and, later, J.J. Homer's Dolphin.

None of the estates, in dealing with development proposals, set their faces against the provision of pubs. Although the Penshurst Arms remains the only Norris pub, it was reported that Henry Norris would in fact have permitted three on his estate. The addition of the Albion to Dupree's existing brewery did not please the Cass trustees, but this must have stemmed more from reaction to its visual impact on what they were designing as the approach to Hackney terrace than from any inherent objection to pubs as such; practically the first lease in Victoria Park road was that of the Sir John Cass in 1852, built by Hughes and taken immediately by Watneys, and no objection was taken to the retention of the Three Mariners when the clearance of the rest of Hackney Bay took place, or indeed its subsequent rebuilding. Other pubs were well distributed around the estate, from the Kenton Arms in Bentham road to the Dagmar arms at the eastern tip. A refusal to allow a pub on Bagge's Harrowgate road land was probably more to do with protecting the tenancy of the Three Mariners than anything else[259].

The Sir John Cass was in the grand style, large and elegant with ample function space as well as two bars; similar was the Cassland Hotel, on the corner of Christie road and Victoria Park road. Most of the other estates were developed on the basis that a pub was a natural part of the scene: the Clarendon Arms on the Parr estate, the Frampton arms; the Bedford Hotel on Thomas Natt's land. On the St Thomas's estate, the only pubs were the surviving Northumberland arms, and the Earl Derby, at

South Hackney chapel, Well street, at the foot of St Thomas's place

the very north eastern, and most meanly built, extremities of the estate's property on Well street and King Edward's road. There was no attempt here to emulate the pub in the grand manner. Something may have been owed to builders' own prejudices[260].

The Crown estate provided pubs liberally, with the Royal, the Royal Standard and the Queen's. Although nothing remains of the pub on William Bradshaw's Grove street development, the rebuilt and re-sited Three Colts ("Public House and Music Hall") graced the west side of Grove street until replaced in the 1880's by the Empress of India[261].

Leaving politics aside, activities available to residents were various clubs, including the Hackney Literary and Scientific Society, co-founded by George Offor junior of Grove street, which met at the Assembly rooms (in Church street, central Hackney). 52 Well street was the home of the Reform Club ("Secretary: Henry Bagg"), and "the Limes" in Cassland road was turned over to club use for a time.

Ample recreation space existed in Victoria Park, where team sports and bathing were popular from an early date; although evidently not space enough to prevent successive grazing tenants of the Common from becoming exasperated by new paths being forged across the field, and subsequently by cricketers pitching their tents. By 1870, the Cass trustees refused to pay rates for the Common, as beneficial occupation had ceased. Other diversions were contemplated, as in the preceding year Oldfield had applied for and been granted permission to use his rope ground for a model railway and tea garden, although nothing seems to have come of this[262].

The impressions of W.S. Clarke were echoed by Henry Currey, when in 1890 he was asked to value the Norris estate: "house property in Hackney has depreciated in value in recent years"[263]. Indeed confidence in the area has never been of the strongest; there have always been too many competitors, too many pressures from the fringes. It would however be difficult to find any area of London to rival the sheer variety of 18th and 19th century styles of building, the contrast of street market and common, palace terrace and parkland, suburbia and light industry: a far from negligible element of the daily enjoyment of living, or retiring there.

Endpiece

Through the investigation of how South Hackney's various surviving building curiosities came about, a number of themes have emerged.

The most consistent is the landowner's motivation for control of what was built on his land. Although it has not been discussed in detail here, when Henry Norris I decided to rebuild his Grove street mansion in 1728, he was able to take advantage of the sophisticated system of building contracts that by that time was well-enough understood in the City by landowners wishing themselves to go into occupation of whatever was built. The Norris contract remains a very early example of a highly developed form of building contract, not only of great detail in the building specifications themselves, but of mechanisms for control of the builder, by means of stage payments, penalties and arbitration[264].

Detailed specifications by developer-landowners, as opposed to occupier-landowners, were themselves known in the City much earlier, yet had appeared to fall into disuse; it is not impossible that standardisation of trade practice and the careful selection of well-established tradesmen made the reduction of standard specifications to writing less necessary, towards the end of the 18th century, than it may have seemed at the beginning. The legislative standardisation imposed incrementally throughout the century, culminating, most notably, in the London Building Act of 1774, must have appeared to make individualised controls, by means of contractual covenants, increasingly otiose. Certainly the Grosvenor estate, in its earliest building agreements of the 1720's, appeared to leave a great deal to be governed by confidence in the person selected as builder.

For whatever reason, it is clear that when in the 1780's they came into the building market, the South Hackney charitable estates had little access to, or interest in, whatever remained available at that time of the professional expertise in building agreements that had undoubtedly existed earlier in the century, and was occasionally applied by developers as much as by intending occupiers. These included the device of holding back the lease itself until substantial work had taken place on the ground. So far as the Cass estate is concerned, once systematic development started the failure to take any contractual control of the building process was evidently swiftly perceived to have been a mistake.

At all events, the mistakes made in the early years of systematic development, when unlicensed sub-letting was a foreseen evil but unlicensed building development was not, have a flavour about them of re-inventing the wheel. Nonetheless the lessons were well learned by those estates that bore them. Control was asserted by those, whether corporate or dynastic, to whom control mattered; the larger, looser organisation such as St Thomas's was less vulnerable, on account of its vast landholdings, from quirks on a particular patch. Thus any residents' objections it received - history does not reveal whether it did - to the encroachment of light industry may have troubled it less, just as it had taken less trouble to prevent it in the first place by careful drafting of leases.

It was inevitable that when they regained possession of their lands after the leases of the 1780's that both St Thomas's and the Cass trustees should look to building development at an early date, and it is interesting that they both anticipated the easing of legal inhibitions on building leases by charities, St Thomas's by several years: it is not clear whether the Hospital's status under royal charter may have been felt to influence this policy. It is curious that when building land was on offer it appeared to be Cass and the Crown estates, and not St Thomas's, that were slow to attract developers, and that when the Cass estate did so it only managed to let building plots in penny numbers, whereas St Thomas's let substantial chunks of ground at a time. This boon was denied to the Cass estate until the 1860's, when pressure of population as much as road and railway routes led the London multitude, for the first time, to beat a path to Hackney.

The more remote situation of the Cass estate undoubtedly influenced its rate of development, but this cannot be the whole explanation, as it may be thought that the Crown estate was as well if not better placed, topographically speaking, as St Thomas's. Furthermore the Crown estate was, at the outset, offering leases of 98 years at least, a length otherwise virtually unknown in South Hackney at the time, certainly for prime sites; and which the Cass trustees consistently avoided, resisting anything in excess of 80 years unless there was no alternative or the builder in question was worth the sacrifice to secure.

The observable trend in the length of leases is interesting. It is clear that during the 18th century a 61 year lease for house building would be the norm, and a 51 year term acceptable. This is quite consistent with the central districts. Although at a relatively early stage the Grosvenor estate was prepared to offer 99 years, and this soon became the central London expectation, central London builders were initially more accustomed to something in the region of the 60 year span, and behaved accordingly. It is difficult to account for the gradual upward trend, other than by way of a growing perception of a common interest between landowner and developer in the investment value of sound building practices and hence a degree of self-interest on both sides.

In Hackney this trend, most readily observable in the St Thomas's leases, which dealt in a wider tract of land than merely South Hackney, and beyond the parish on the Tyssen estate, led to the commonplace 61 years of the late 18th century reaching 80 years in the 1840's, and only exceptionally longer; till at the end of the century 90 years and upwards appears to have become the acceptable minimum to the intending builder.

Perceptible, if elusive, as a visual result of the configuration of landownership, is the effect that substantial co-operation between owners had on the layout of streets. It is only necessary to ask, to demonstrate this, what would have been the consequence of a refusal by the Hicklings or the Reas to open up King Edward's or Victoria Park roads, or the Norrises to part with the Alexandra site. The impact of such a fantasy is however reduced by the post-war obliteration of much that had been achieved in rational street planning, and the inevitable wiping out through bombing and otherwise of clues which might have unlocked further nuances in the language of building development.

Perceptible also is the fact of the smaller-scale, more densely built houses being concentrated on the smaller estates, such as Bradshaw's, Hedger's and Parr's. The perception of the perpetual nature of their interest influenced the charitable estates towards building large and building substantially. At the same time, the very existence of their smaller competitors, more interested in a quick return, must have inhibited the likely success of such a policy.

It is difficult now, with only patchy surviving photographic evidence of the vanished bulk of the St Thomas's estate, to gauge with any confidence the comparative value of the contribution made to the Cass estate by the presence of a resident surveyor. The photographic evidence suggests that the St Thomas's builders were not innovative architects, which within his limitations George Wales was; but those limitations included restriction of his influence where the developer was acting as his own architect.

Undoubtedly in estate management terms, notably in the considerable workload generated by rack-renting and modernising Hackney terrace and its troublesome Lawn, many problems will have been nipped in the bud by the surveyor's imminent presence. Perhaps the personalities involved generated other problems.

Given, however, that the estate was consistently disadvantaged in competitive terms, giving rise in the first fifteen years of serious development to a plethora of minor, two to three plot building agreements, it is difficult to imagine that such coherence as it has could have been as readily achieved had George Wales also been employed, say, on major central London or Devonshire estate building projects to the same extent as his counterpart Henry Currey, instead of living amongst it all next to the Cassland estate office. Equally, one may ask, in what way would the present appearance of the streets have been different had Wales and Clark not, however unwisely, aligned their own financial interests so closely with the estate's. There is no doubt but that they sought for it the highest achievable standards of building and design, and even the most suspect dealing is capable of the explanation that it was in pursuit of the abortive plan to co-ordinate street alignments with Frampton Park.

Amongst the smaller estates (in which we may include for this purpose the Jackson underlease of 1790 on the Cass estate) the influence of what might be called "building by subscription" is notable. Hackney terrace was not unique, but it has not proved possible to identify comparable and roughly contemporary developments, other than the Pollard's row enterprise, a product of the same minds; or provincial building society projects, from which there are significant differences in social, financial and architectural terms.

Equally, the Brookfield road and Hickling estate developments are not unique, but they have features of significant interest. Like Cassland crescent, the variance of architectural styles in the former gives concrete and visual evidence of the building recession of the 1850's. Visually the latter defies the effects of that recession, and also offers a telling contrast with Brookfield road in its thoroughly urban character - a character not normally pursued with any architectural deliberation by the Freehold Land fraternity who conceived it, who were just as capable of creating semi-detached cottages where that was what the market wanted (as at Wembley) as they were of creating city streets (as in Hackney or Kentish Town or the Potteries of Notting Hill).

The subscribers, certainly no less than building developers, would always vote with their feet; and out of Hackney they wanted different things. For the earliest, escape from the City's crowds and smells without an escape from City styles. Later, for some, Hackney was still a village on the City's fringe, for others a more remote but still urban adjunct of the familiar. Undoubtedly, had they had the market in their favour, the larger estates would in their period of systematic development have cultivated the Hackney of the suburban villa, capitalising on the Park and the Common: Cassland crescent and King Edward's road set the tone.

After the mid 1850's, which not only saw the inception of Hedger's minor urban streets, following on from Parr, Bradshaw and Matthews, but the bland terraced frontages of Frampton Park, it was clear that the city had won. Echoing the Norris estate, the northern and eastern Cass estate mass builders developed a kind of urban terrace whose bow fronts, down to the 1890's, pay homage to the villas they might have preferred to be. And yet to this day its setting in park and common makes South Hackney both city and country: "urbs in rure".

APPENDIX 1

Glossary of street names

Old name:	Location or present name
Bishop road:	Killowen road
Blenheim cottages:	1-7 Church crescent
Brampton road:	Bramshaw road
Broadway:	Lauriston road, south of Victoria park road
Cassland crescent:	11-35 Cassland road
Church street:	Mare street, north
Dagmar road:	Danesdale road
Glaskin road:	ran north from Well street, opposite no.60
Gotha street:	Warneford street, east/west section
Greenwood's row:	Kingshold road
Grove street:	Lauriston road (east of present line insofar as north of Victoria park road)
Grove street lane:	Victoria Park road, east of Lauriston road
Grove villas:	Victoria Park road, north side, between Gascoyne road and six houses east of Dagmar road
Hackney terrace:	20-54 Cassland road (even numbers)
Havelock road:	ran north from Well street, opposite no.76
King Edward's road:	King Edward's road (west); Moulins road (east); centre section under Kingshold estate
Manor road:	Holcroft road
New Church road:	Balcorne street
North street:	Northiam Street
Paragon:	Paragon road, north side
Park place:	opposite 1-7 Church crescent
Park street:	Fremont street
Percy road:	Kingshold road
Providence row:	part of Wetherell road
St. Thomas's road:	Ainsworth road (north); Skipworth road (south)

Shore place:	Shore road
Silk Mill row:	cottages at east end of Cassland road (north side, opposite Brookfield road)
Spackman's buildings:	244-252 Mare street
Terrace road west:	Elsdale street
Tryon's place:	Tudor road, west of nos. 14-28
Tryon's terrace:	14-28 Tudor road
Union road:	Bradstock road
Victoria grove:	ran north from Morpeth road
Victoria street:	Warneford street
Water gruel row:	cottages to the east of Shore road

APPENDIX 2

Buiders and speculators, 1845-1900:
Biographical notes

These notes have been compiled principally from applications for approval of plans to build and drain made to the Hackney Board of Works from 1855 onwards; registered memorials in the Middlesex Deeds register; registers of leases by St Thomas's Hospital, Sir John Cass's Charity estate and the Crown estate; Norris estate papers; family sources; census returns, probate records and commercial directories.

ADAMS AND SON
of Ealing; built 335-9 Victoria Park road (demolished) on the Brookfield road estate, from 1864.
ALLEN, HENRY ROBERT
Born Chelsea, c. 1833. Builder, of 19 Sewardstone road (1861-3), later of 11, Annis road (1868), and 319 Victoria park road (1890: by this time he describes himself as a surveyor). After building on the Frampton Park estate (Cf BUTTERS, GLASKIN) he collaborated with T.P. Glaskin and John WRIGHT on the former's Dagmar road property of 1858, then on the latter's 1864 agreement for adjacent land, building much of Dagmar road under Wright's agreement with Glaskin and part of the Victoria park road frontages on both developments, 1862-63. In 1870 he took agreements for leases of 26 houses on Crown land in Cadogan terrace, eventually himself leasing nos. 16-28; about this time his permanent workforce was 6 men and 4 boys.
AUBYN, HENRY
Builder of Mile End terrace, Canal road, Stepney; built 2 houses in Gotha street, 1862.
AVENELL, WILLIAM J.
Timber merchant of Squirries street, Bethnal Green, who in 1854 entered into a building agreement with the Cass trustees, leading to his lease of 81 and 83 Victoria Park road; he may have intended to develop neighbouring land, but did not do so. In 1872 at 1, Marriot terrace, Lower Clapton road.
In 1867, of Osmond House, built by A. BORTON on Crown land.
BAGGE,HENRY
bricklayer turned master builder, born Shipdham, Norfolk, c. 1822. In 1859/60, taking leases of houses in Glaskin road, sub-contracting from T.P. Glaskin and Charles Butters in their development of the Frampton estate. From 1861, active with Robert MORLEY first as neighbouring builders on the Frampton estate, then in St Thomas's road under William NORRIS's agreement with St Thomas's Hospital; then, from 1862, in partnership under a building agreement with Henry Norris V for development on 80 year leases of his estate west of Lauriston road, together with the frontage on the eastern side of that road. In the following year, undertook a building agreement with the Cass trustees for 80 year leases in Harrowgate road, and in 1864 developed the Grove street lane frontage of Banbury road. Developer/builder of 2 large detached villas and 2 others in Gore road, 1868. Resident 1959-1862 in Glaskin road, thereafter at 1, Speldhurst road.
BAGGE, CHARLES and ROBERT
of Percy road, building contractors from HENRY BAGGE in Harrowgate road, 1864-5.
BARSHT, ARTHUR
Developer of the site of "the Limes", 7 Cassland road, 1900. Address at 106 Cheapside.

BANKS, ROBERT THOMAS of Dagmar terrace. Building contractor for WRIGHT <N>in Dagmar road and Christie road, 1864. Building in Bentham road in 1867 (houses now demolished).

BEAN, MARK
c.1860-7, plumber and glazier at 181 Mile End road. Building contractor for R.E. BORTON in Cornwall and Rutland roads, 1864-5; leased houses in Cawley road (1874) and Gore road (1875) from the Crown.

BECKETT, GEORGE
builder, of Kenton lodge, Kenton road, where he built at least nos. 2-4, and 2-10 Brampton road, on building agreements of 1864 and 1870. In 1883, of Staples road, Loughton, Essex.

BEETLES, JOHN WILLIAM
Builder. In 1866 built 2 houses in Well street and Denmark villas in Shore road, on St Thomas's hospital land. Cf. NORRIS, William.

BISHOP, BENJAMIN
Builder, of 7 Barry street, New North road; sub-contractor to BAGGE and MORLEY in Southborough and Lauriston roads (1862-6), and 203-11 Victoria park road (1864).

BISHOP, GEORGE
Builder and developer, of Coleman street, Islington. In 1862-3, participated with HARMAN in building on lease from St Thomas's Hospital of land in Darnley road; subsequently contracted for development of Poole's charity estate (Poole, Valentine and Bishop roads, with west side Queen Anne road and part of Well street), and adjacent Cass properties (in the eastern part of Cassland crescent); completed 1867. In 1867 based in Denmark cottages, Well street; in 1872 at 1 Cassland villas (11 Cassland road).

BLACKMORE, THOMAS
Of Park place, South Hackney. Sub-contractor from WILLIAM NORRIS under the latter's 1859 agreement with St Thomas's Hospital, building at least 11 houses in King Edward's road in 1862. After an abortive agreement for building, on his own account, 3 houses in Cassland road (nos. 41-5, 1867) became a foreman involved in building Gore road for S. Barnett.

BOREHAM, JAMES
Of Barnards place, Holloway; sub-contractor for BAGGE and MORLEY in Southborough road.

BORTON, ALFRED
builder, of 33 Rutland road. Built now-demolished houses on Crown estate in Wetherell road, and Victoria Park road, from 1865-8; in Gore road in 1875.

BORTON, RICHARD EDWARD
Born c. 1819, in Bethnal Green. Plumber, in 1860 at 103 Bethnal green road; in 1861 at Bishopsgate street, subsequently of Victoria Park road, where in 1860 he began the first significant development of the Crown's South Hackney estate, having previously built houses in Approach road on the Bethnal green side. His work included nos.58-82 Victoria park road and the Royal and the Royal Standard pubs, both designed by Joseph Harris. In 1862, describing himself for census purposes as a "retired plumber", he concluded an agreement with the Cass estate for the development of Derby and Rutland roads, on 90 year leases. Also resident at Hillside, Farningham, Kent. He died in 1877, leaving something less than £12,000.

BUCKINGHAM, THOMAS
Of Holly street, Dalston. Acted for EASTMAN on his developments in Victoria park road, 1860-2. In 1861, applied for approval of building plans at 29 Downs road.

BUTTERS, CHARLES
Born in Harling, Norfolk, 1807; a carpenter by trade, establishing a building yard in London c. 1830. His wife was Elizabeth Plain. His first building agreement with St Thomas's Hospital was for a "strip of land" in King Edward's road in 1847; in the following year he made with the Governors of the Hospital a substantial building agreement for 75 year leases in Shore road and King Edward's road, developed over the next 15 years. He himself went into residence at Shore road and subsequently Parkfield villa, 41 King Edward's road, one of the development's most substantial houses, originally built for THOMAS KELSEY, via 48 Well street (Norfolk house).

(Norfolk house). Other building in Well street and Shore road took place under agreements of 1852 and 1854. About this time his permanent workforce consisted of about 12 men. In 1856, with his financier T.P.GLASKIN, he undertook development of the entire Frampton estate, with which this partnership's agreement of 1859 for part of the St Thomas's estate north of Well street (chiefly in Darnley road) was usefully connected. The partnership were also active at the same time on the Warburton estate west of Mare street. A prominent churchman and poor law guardian, and a member of the Vestry though not the Board of Works (cf. GLASKIN), he died in 1889, leaving some £21,000. His son Walter, (1839-1906) was also a builder (at Tite road on the St Thomas's estate at Lower Clapton) and resident in King Edward's road; he married Annie Offor, daughter of George Offor of Grove street, bookseller, magistrate and member of the Metropolitan Board of Works. A grand-daughter married James HARMAN junior. The building firm founded by Charles and Walter Butters and later taken over by others was active in South Hackney well into this century, having premises in Warneford street.

CATLING, GEORGE and JAMES
George Catling (c. 1803-94) was born in Godmanchester. A carpenter, of Satchwell's Rents, Bethnal Green road, a business subsequently carried on by his son JAMES, he built and leased in 1855/6 a house facing Victoria Park road and backing onto Well street common, to the east of the later Queen's Gate villas; this he called Brampton cottage. Ostensibly retired as a carpenter by 1861, the firm remained active in taking agreements of building land from the Cass estate in Brampton road (1862, houses now demolished) and Union road, building in Cassland road (1864 onwards); his address in 1890 was 51 Cassland road, and the terrace eastwards from this to no. 57 is of Catling construction.

CLARK, JOHN
Solicitor; Registrar to Sir John Cass charity. Building agreements 1847 for Blenheim cottages with Monger's trustees (lease assignee 1854);1852 for 38-44 Terrace road and 9-11 Cassland road. He died in 1854, his widow, Martha Clark, investing and living in Glaskin and Allen's Grove villas.

COBELDICK, JOHN
With MARGETTS, a sub-contractor to BAGGE in Victoria park road, 1865.

COCKERELL, CHARLES
Builder of 209-11 and 217-9 Victoria park road, on lease from Henry Norris, from 1862.

COLE, EDWARD
Of Radnor terrace, Ballspond road; builder of houses in Victoria grove, 1862.

COOK, WILLIAM
undertaker, of 3 Church street, Mile End. In 1853, completed (at least in part) houses (demolished) on the corner of Grove street and Terrace road; having been noted as getting into difficulties by the Cass estate.

CURREY, HENRY
The first of three members of his family to act as surveyors to St Thomas's Hospital, he was responsible for the design of the new hospital buildings at Vauxhall (1865), as well as for much building on the Devonshire estates, relatives of his being this estate's legal advisers. (The Dukes of Devonshire and their gardener Paxton were patrons of Loddiges' nursery on St Thomas's land.) Currey designed the St Thomas's estate layouts, the southern estate at the latest in 1850 and the northern at the end of the Loddiges lease in 1856; also a sketch for the Norris estate in 1850. He was commissioned to design the new parochial school on its removal from Grove street in 1847. His office also performed routine applications for drainage work on the St Thomas's estate. e g for JAMES HARMAN in Tite road.

DABELL, JOSEPH
Mason; builder in Warneford street; of Salisbury crescent, Agar Town.

DAY, GEORGE
Active as a South Hackney builder 1854-6, when from premises in Bentham road (probably no.2), he produced the Kenton Arms, 36 Kenton road, and houses on the now demolished north side of

Bentham road, as well as at least 7 Cassland crescent for THOMAS GILLESPY, and probably the remainder of 13-23 Cassland road.

DEAN, JOHN
Of Old Ford. Built 6 houses in Cadogan terrace, 1862.

DYER, WILLIAM BARRETT
Born c. 1831 in Cornwall. Builder, of 1 Stafford road, Tredegar road, Bow. Developed Shafton road on 80 year leases from 1868, Ruthven street and the Grove street lane frontage on this south side from 1871/2. In 1878, resident at 6 Rockmead road, which road he was responsible for building at least in part in 1874, he was building actively in Glyn road, Clapton; he died in 1896 while resident in Gascoyne road, leaving leasehold estate at Walthamstow.

EASTMAN, HUGH THOMAS
Born c.1818 in Camberwell. First traceable in Hackney to Hackney terrace, where in 1853 he was briefly resident, by 1856 he was established in Navarino road, where he described himself variously as a "merchant" or "iron agent". In that year he financed the building of villas in Eleanor road. From 1860-3 he developed a large tranche of Cass and Norris land on the northern side of Victoria Park road, from Fremont street eastwards, including the four long terraces west of the roundabout. During the 1860's he operated as a surveyor,from offices in Gracechurch street, from about 1873 adding "architect" to his self-description of "surveyor". By 1877 he had removed to Anerley.

EDWARDS, ROBERT
Builder of 3-8 Queen Anne road, 1865; 13 Union road, 1867; active also in Bentham road, 1867.

ELLIS, JOHN
of Trinity Square, Brixton; builder, west side Homer road, 1863.

ENNOR, THOMAS
Builder, of Commercial road east, Stepney. In 1862-3, built 1-8 St Agnes terrace. Built the Queen's Hotel (the Falcon & Firkin)in 1865, and the Bedford Hotel, Wetherell road in pursuance of an application to build and drain of 1866.

FEAST, WILLIAM
1859-71, a carpenter resident in Victoria (Warneford) street, responsible for building on the St Pancras, Marylebone and Paddington Freehold Land Society estate, nos. 20-22 King Edward's road, and houses in Warneford street. In 1871, employed one man and one boy.

GARDNER, THOMAS
of Tonbridge place, King's Cross. In 1856 built 2 pairs of semi's on the S.V.V.A. estate's Victoria park road frontage; in 1860, concerned in building part of Hedger's grove.

GILLESPY, THOMAS
Born Shoreditch, c. 1792. A ship and insurance broker, resident in Woburn place, Well street, and later in St Thomas's road. In 1855 and 1857, an investor in King Edward's road; in 1856, sponsored building of 13-21 and probably also 23 Cassland road. Active in parish affairs, including the building of the Norris almshouses. He was evidently a respected figure in the community, being elected auditor by the first Hackney vestry in 1855. He died in 1872.

GLASKIN, THOMAS PEET
Born c. 1813 in Bethnal Green, Glaskin was originally in business as a silk net manufacturer. By 1854 Glaskin was underleasing part of BUTTERS's building land on the east side of Shore road, where he moved in in 1856 to no. 26, which the latter built for him, subsequently developing the garden of this plot himself, probably with the builder's assistance. In 1856-7 this partnership laid out the Frampton estate, complete by 1860; Glaskin alone seems to have been involved with the Homer estate, in support of his development of which he took the land that subsequently became Dagmar road. In the early 1860's, again in concert with Butters, he was active on the Warburton estate, near London Fields; in Spurstowe road; and later at Lower Clapton, this time again on St Thomas's land, around Tite and Comberton roads. After 1867, Glaskin moved to Manor villas, Amherst road, part of which road, with part of Pembury road, he was responsible for building (the sewers were a joint effort with HARMAN). A member of the Hackney vestry instituted in

1855, he failed to secure the election of himself, CHARLES BUTTERS and RAYNER to the Board of Works.

GOODMAN, JAMES AND JOSIAH
Builders, of Grove road, Mile End, later 256 Green street, Bethnal green, and Cumberland wharf. Leased houses on the Bethnal Green side of the Crown Victoria Park estate in 1861. As well as sub-contracting from R. E. BORTON in Derby and Rutland roads, 1863, developed Meynell road and the associated Cassland road frontage from 1875-9, and in Bentham road in 1881. Were active on the Tredegar estate, Bow, including in Ordell road, 1868.

HARMAN, JAMES
Harman's money came from an ironmongery business at 136-8 St John's road, Hoxton, which enabled him to buy a residence (or residences) with grounds at Willesden and known as Willesden House or Stonebridge Park House; later he lived at Milton, near Gravesend. Amongst his other activities was a trusteeship of the West London and General Permanent Building Society. As lessee, he is described as an ironmonger; in directing the disposal to others of leases to which he is entitled, he is described as a builder; in granting underleases, he describes himself as a gentleman. He had property interests in Kilburn and Shoreditch (Harman street) as well as Willesden and Hackney. His first dealings in Hackney seem to have been under building agreements of 1859 for the Darnley road/Paragon road part of the St Thomas's estate; his incursions onto the Homer estate came in 1861. In 1863 he had a base in Graham road, and was building on the Clapton estate belonging to St Thomas's hospital. His major development in South Hackney was as developer on the whole of the Norris estate east of Bagge and Morley's Lauriston road frontages (other than the site of the French Hospital). Subsequently associated with GLASKIN in relation to a sewerage application for Amherst road.

HAYNES, J
Builder, of 5 Liverpool road, Islington; 1857-60, built nos. 10-14 even Victoria (Warneford) Street, 1858-63.

HOMER, JOHN JAMES and RICHARD
J.J. Homer was born c.1810, in Wandsworth. The brothers were publicans, of the Dolphin, Mare street; developed the Mills field east of Brookfield road on lease, part sub-letting to HARMAN and GLASKIN. J.J. Homer was active in parish affairs, being the first chairman of the Norris almshouses management committee, and a vestryman.

HONEYWILL, SILAS
Builder in Warneford street, 1856, and (on a larger scale) in Southgate and Englefield roads. A vestryman of this surname was elected in 1855.

HORN, JOHN
of Hedgers Grove, 1861, where he built nos. 1-11.

HUGHES, JAMES ALEXANDER
Builder, of Enfield road north, De Beauvoir Town. Building agreement, 1851, for extensive land in Victoria Park road; completed by mortgagees under notice from the Cass estate. Constructed the Sir John Cass public house; also 1-5 Cassland road, 1851/2.

INNES, JAMES and JOHN
Merchants, of Mincing lane. Between 1860 and 1862 they financed nos. 4-28 Bentham road, in 1868 taking a further lease of the corner plot [Gloucester road]. Saw themselves as "wholesalers" in land; it is not clear what relationship they assumed with the City builders employed in building the first Bentham road terraces or local small builders who finished off their contract land in and near this road.

JACKSON, GEORGE
A professional house investor, born c. 1783; possibly an heir to James Jackson's Hackney terrace leases of 1796. Apparently a developer or sub-contractor from Page in Terrace road west, 1852; financed the building of 6-10 Cassland road, 1852 (cf KELSEY).

126

JARVIS, JAMES
Builder, of Forest road, Dalston (1866), possibly subsequently of 31 Hassett road. Sub-contractor
from James Harman on the eastern Norris estate, 1864-6; at the same time active in Lansdowne
road.
KELLY, THOMAS FITZROY
Of Castle Kelly, Co. Cork, where he was born c. 1810; possibly formerly active in Holborn,
Shoreditch and Hampton Wick; by 1860, of Culford road, de Beauvoir town. His building
agreement with the Cass trustees for land on the south side of Victoria park road (nos. 98-162
even) west of the Alexandra pub in 1862 was completed over 10 years; he built no. 126,
Alexandra house, for himself. At the same time he was building also in de Beauvoir road. He had
some trouble with the Cass estate, having built unauthorised stabling at the back of the
Alexandra; they refused him a further agreement on the northern estate but subsequently let the
east side of Brampton road (1874). Of White Point house, Queenstown, Ireland; died 1889.
KELSEY, THOMAS
Born Middlesex, c.1823. Silk manufacturer of Milk street, City and Wilmot square, Bethnal Green,
employing a workforce of 300. Resident c.1850 of Hackney terrace, subsequently of one of the
largest houses in King Edward's road, where he was an investor in leases, and where Henry and
George Kelsey, trimming manufacturer and a silk merchant, were also resident, in neighbouring
Parkfield terrace. Financed 12-16 Cassland road, 1852 (cf JACKSON), and 1 Manor road, before
1859, getting into difficulties in connection with the latter and being released from subsequent
building agreements.
KIMBER, JAMES
A sub-contractor in King Edward's road from NORRIS, and in Paragon place; also active in
Graham road.
KITTERIDGE, ROBERT HILL
Born c.1815, in Linton, Cambridgeshire. Probably the son of the Robert Kitteridge, carpenter of
Homerton, who built on the north side of Dalston lane on building lease from W.G.D. Tyssen in
1824. Himself a carpenter/cabinet maker, of Well street, then Kenton road, where in 1857/8 he
built nos. 18-22, using the backland originally as a builder's yard. He appears to have been at
least the principal builder of Charles terrace, Cassland road in 1858-60, for the LEFEVERS,
underleasing from them with the help of building society finance.
LAVERS, WILLIAM
Builder, of Stamford place, Acton street, Kingsland, subsequently of 32 Southborough, then
Groombridge road. Substantial sub-contractor for Bagge and Morley on the Norris estate
(Speldhurst road, 1862), Southborough road (1864), Lauriston road (1864-5); from T. P. Glaskin in
Amherst road (Manor place 1868); and from Harman in Kilburn.
LEFEVER, CHARLES (ELDER & YOUNGER)
Both mathematical instrument makers, resident in Highbury and London Fields respectively,
who were active in developing a terrace in Cassland road (called Charles terrace: see also
KITTERIDGE) and the east side of Bradstock road, on 80 year leases from 1857, work which was
substantially complete in 1858.
LEWIS, EVAN
Born in Cardiganshire, c. 1838. Builder, of 34 Annis road and 62 Christie road, active in sub-
contracting from John Wright in Annis and Christie roads, and developing small plots in
Brampton and Gloucester road (1866-7) and 59-73 Cassland road with the west side of Kenton
road (1869-71) on his own account. Died 1884.
LUCAS, JOSEPH
Builder, 30 Approach road, Bethnal Green.Partner or sub-contractor with R.E. BORTON on the
latter's agreement of 1862 with the Cass trustees for Derby and Rutland roads. Subsequently of
Addington road, Bow; a developer on the Tredegar estate, 1868; sub-contracted from the
GOODMANS in Meynell/Cassland roads in 1875-9. Builder in Rockmead/Cawley roads, 1874-5.
MARGETTS, HENRY: see COBELDICK.

MARTIN, STEPHEN,
of Wilton road, Dalston. From 1864, developed land in Penshurst and Groombridge road. From 1867, working on Manor villas, Amherst road (cf GLASKIN, HARMAN).

MATE, JOHN
Police sergeant, Well street, and developer (1852) of 47-9 Balcorne street.

MATTHEWS, MARMADUKE
Auctioneer and surveyor resident at Spital square and then at Cambridge lodge, Mare street. Bought land in Wick road, developed from 1860. Sold the backland of his house for the Congregational church; built Cambridge lodge villas adjacent.

MELDRUM, PHILIP
Builder, of Salmon lane, Limehouse. Built 59-61 St Thomas's road in 1861; built Cintra villas on the north side of Victoria park road in 1862/3; built most of the east side of Queen Anne road, 1868, removing his business there. Died c.1868.

MORLEY, ROBERT
Born Marston, Lincolnshire, c. 1822. Carpenter; active on Frampton park estate contemporarily with Henry BAGGE. With him took building agreement from Henry Norris V in 1862. In 1861 employed 12 men.

NAGLE, GARRETT
Born c. 1811, in Ireland. Builder, of Brighton place, Hackney road, participating in Bradshaw's development near Victoria Park c. 1846. The builder of 54 Victoria Park road, "Charlotte house", as his own residence, leased to him in 1860.

NEWMAN, EDWARD
of Orchard st, Old Ford; in 1860, involved in building part of Hedger's grove. A sub-contractor from BAGGE in Harrowgate road, he built 134-8 Cassland road, 1864.

NORRIS, WILLIAM
born 1805/6, Potters Bar/South Mimms, Middlesex, son of a wheelwright, later of Cheshunt; married (1834) Eleanor (Catherine), daughter of John Murray, bookseller and stationer of Coventry street. Trained as a carpenter, he was active as a builder in Hackney by 1841, having premises in Mare street, near the Triangle, in or near which he also lived, moving subsequently to premises of his own building in Shore road, then to Well street (no. [74]) and Ainsworth road (no.31). Apparently he contracted for the carpentry in the new church of St John of Jerusalem, c.1847, and for supplementary building works on the Norris almshouses in 1855. His most significant building work was on the St Thomas's Hospital estate, with major building agreements for 80 year leases of the west side of Shore road (1851 and 1854), the east side of St Thomas's road (1859) and the whole eastern segment of King Edward's road to the estate boundary, including the west side of Handley road and Speldhurst road. In 1851 his staff consisted of 65 men. His son Henry followed him into the business, which is shown in 1872 as occupying premises at 1, St Thomas's place. He also dealt in land, buying a lease of nos. 3-15 Cambridge terrace from William Rea in 1850, assigning the lease in 1863. By 1861 he had apparently retired from the building business; he was active as a vestryman during the following decade (defeating BUTTERS, GLASKIN and RAYNER for a place on the Board of Works in 1855). He died at 31 Ainsworth road in 1877, leaving an estate of some £2,000.

OLDFIELD, GEORGE
Of Chard, Somerset; established the "Cassland ropeworks" north of Bentham road, having advertised for suitable land in the press in May 1848. Developed much of the north side of Bentham road, and Chard villas in Kenton road). Died in 1882.

PAGE, JOHN
Builder, of Albany road, Barnsbury Park; built in Terrace road (he called part of it Albany place) from 1851-4, and Terrace road west (Page's cottages), and Well street, including 132-158; partly financed by G.R. WALES. Possibly the builder of the same name operating c.1860 from South Molton street.

PEARSON, JOHN
Developer; took a building agreement 1851 with St Thomas's Hospital for west side of St Thomas's road, dying shortly thereafter.

PHILLIPS, NICHOLAS and RICHARD
A plumber, of Homerton, and a relative, of Clarendon square, Somers town (the "Polygon"). Built 4 terraced houses in Union road, 1856/7.

PILGRIM, ABEL
Builder; in 1858-9, leased land and houses in Loddiges road, Stanley road and on both sides of Frampton Park road from St Thomas's Hospital; here he established his business. Also subcontracted for William Norris in St Thomas's road, and on the Norris estate, where he defaulted on a building society mortgage in King Edward's road, 1864.

PRICE, HENRY
Builder, of 35 Cambridge terrace, Loddiges road. A sub-contractor from BAGGE and MORLEY in Southborough road, underleasing in 1863; and in King Edward's road on the Norris estate, undertaking general building in 1865.

RABY, JAMES
Builder, of Weymouth terrace, Hackney road. In 1856, built 4 to 8 and 35 Brookfield road, and in 1862 a house in Handley road. Later, lived in Ockendon road, Canonbury.

RAYNER, WILLIAM, jr.
Born in Bethnal Green, c.1807.Both a sub-contractor and principal contractor under 75-year building agreements on the St Thomas's Hospital estate in Tryon's place and King Edward's road, 1851-4; operating from Cambridge terrace at this time. By 1856 he was active on the northern St Thomas's hospital estate, where he developed, inter alia, Rayner street (now demolished); and on the Frampton estate, e g in Havelock road. Resident in Havelock villa, King Edward's road; in 1861 he was employing some 10 men. In this year he built the St Thomas's hall on the east side of St Thomas's road. In 1865, took a lease for 80 years from 1862 of land in Shore road from the St Thomas's Hospital estate. In 1875, he was resident at 114 Graham road. A vestryman, like his associates BUTTERS and GLASKIN he was unsuccessful in gaining election to the Board of Works.

REDGRAVE, WILLIAM
Builder, of 14 Homerton terrace. In 1862-3, built shops on the east side of Grove street; also, from 1863, in Kenton road and Wick road (now demolished). Built shops on the south side of Grove street lane, near the roundabout, 1864-5.

REEVE, ROBERT
Of 1 High street, Stoke Newington. Sub-contractor from BAGGE and MORLEY on the Norris estate, in Southborough and Lauriston roads.

REYNOLDS, CHARLES
Undertaker, 11 Plumber street, City road. Sub-contractor from BAGGE and MORLEY in Speldhurst road, 1862.

SAUNDERS AND FIELD
Builders of Underwood street, Mile End New Town; builders in St Thomas's road, 1862, Victoria Park road (123-7), 1862-3.

SCHOLTES, JOHN
In 1859-62, of Glaskin road; sub-contractor, 1863-5, in Southborough and Lauriston roads from BAGGE and MORLEY; also built part of the Victoria Park road frontage, leasing no. 217-9. In 1872-5, built 30-42 Bentham road and 12-16 Brampton (his own premises being at no. 16) for INNES.

SHEARMAN, WILLIAM
Builder, Dagmar road, 1864. Died 1870.

SKINNER, FRANCIS and ALFRED
Of Lower Clapton. Built a terrace of small houses in Well street (Tesco's site), 1862/3.

SMITH, ALFRED and JOB
of Worship street; substantial building (now demolished) in Bentham and Gloucester roads, 1867 onwards.

THOMERSON, WILLIAM
Born Essex, c.1798; of Hackney road, builder, then of "Chesnut cottage, Shore road"; developer of the south western corner of the Parr estate, including Balcorne street.

TRUMAN, JOSEPH
of Hockley street, Homerton; builder of 91-7 Cassland road (where he lived at 91), 1861 onwards.

TUCKER, SAMUEL and SAMUEL JOEL
Father and son, born c. 1800 and 1827, in Devonshire. Bricklayers. Sub-contractors, c.1862, in Speldhurst road, on NORRIS's 1859 building agreement with St Thomas's Hospital; builders of 2 pairs of semi's in Gascoyne road, 1869/70. In 1870, established at 26 Queen Anne road; the workforce about this time was 10 men and 3 boys. Built 23-25 Queen Anne road, also in Union road, and as sub-contractors for G. J. BISHOP.

TURNER, WILLIAM
Carpenter, of Hackney road and Queensbridge road, variously given as born in Maldon, c. 1810, and in Cambridge, c. 1822. In 1854-5, built 13-21 Holcroft road, in 1861, 14-20 St Thomas's road; in 1862, houses in Greenwood row and Paragon road. In 1862, took leases from St Thomas's Hospital of houses in Stanley road and St Thomas's road, the former in pursuance of PEARSON'S agreement of 1851 and followed by further completions there and on the Well street frontage let under the same agreement, in 1867 and 1871. A substantial sub-contractor from HARMAN in Penshurst and Southborough road (east), 1866-7; built 223-243 Victoria park road. Resident previously at 19 Holcroft road ("Clarendon cottage"), in 1871 he is at the Cedars, Banbury road.

WALES, GEORGE RICHARD
Born c.1818 in Middlesex, son of George Richmond Wales, house proprietor, of Norfolk, St John's Wood and ultimately South Hackney. Appointed surveyor to the Cass charity estate in 1845; resigned 1863. Also operated as a surveyor from Great St Helens, Bishopsgate, while living at Cassland house, next to the estate office, at the west end of Hackney terrace. The architect of Monger s rebuilt almshouses and 1-7 Church crescent (1847-8); probably also of 38-44 Terrace road, 6-16 Cassland road, and 81-7 and 97-119 Victoria Park road. Heavily involved in financing the builders DAY and PAGE. Active in developments at Clapton and as developer's surveyor on the Poole estate, 1867-8; advised the Cass estate on rebuilding the Aldgate schoolhouse, 1868. A member of the Hackney vestry at its inception in 1855. Possibly the George Wales operating as a builder at 36 Kenton road in 1890-6, leasing land at Carlton road and Daubeny road, Clapton.

WHEEN, GEORGE
Of Lower street (Essex road) Islington; applied for building approval for 11-14 St Thomas's place, 1858.

WILLMOTT, EDWARD JAMES
Builder, West street, Triangle. Built 12 houses (347-369 odd) in Victoria park road, known as Homer terrace, and 13-21 St Thomas's road from 1860, 18 King Edward's road in 1861 and 5-11 Shore road (demolished) in 1862.

WINKLEY, HENRY AND CHARLES
Developers of Queen's Gate villas, 1891, and Meynell crescent, 1894. Both subsequently resident in Meynell crescent. A Charles Winkley was mayor of Hackney in 1914.

WRIGHT, JOHN
Builder, of West street, The Triangle. Active in Glaskin road, 1861/2; took over GLASKIN's brickfield at Hackney Wick, from 1864, in which year entered into an agreement with the Cass trustees for 150 houses at Annis and Christie roads.

WRIGHT, ROBERT and THOMAS
builders' merchants, Old Ford road, Bethnal Green. Financed DYER in the development of Shafton road and Minson roads, 1867-8.

Sources

For the Cass estate, the principal source has been the Sir John Cass Foundation's minute books, both those of the Governors and of their Hackney Estates Committee; and miscellaneous unlisted building agreements. The Norris estate papers are in Hackney Archives Department. The estate papers for St Thomas's Hospital are at the Greater London Record Office, where records of Valentine Poole's charity, the Norris almshouses and the 19th century administration of Monger's charity are in the parish charity series. That Office also has the papers of the Commissioners of Woods and Forests relating to Victoria Park, including some relating to the land acquisition; development of the Crown estate for building is recorded principally amongst the Land Revenues series at the Public Record Office, Chancery lane.

Much use has also been made of the Middlesex Deeds Register at the GLRO. Miscellaneous manuscripts in the Guildhall and Tower Hamlets collections have also been consulted, as noted. For the operations of the St Pancras, Marylebone and Paddington Freehold Land Society, resort has also been had to material in the British Library (Newspapers) and several local London collections, notably that at the Marylebone Library. Material relating to the French Hospital is in the Library of the Huguenot Society.

Abbreviations in the footnotes are as follows:-

D/F/NOR	Norris estate papers, at HAD
GLRO	Greater London Record Office
HAD	Hackney Archives Department
H1/ST/E	St Thomas's Hospital estate papers, at GLRO
HL	Huguenot Library
JCB	Sir John Cass Foundation building agreements, leases etc. (mostly unlisted)
JCM	minutes of the Governors of the Sir John Cass foundation, or their Hackney Estates Committee.
MDR	Middlesex Deeds Register
PRO	Public Record Office
VPP	Victoria Park Papers, at GLRO
Robinson	History and Antiquities of Hackney, William Robinson, 2 vols. (1843)
Clarke	Glimpses of Ancient Hackney and Stoke Newington, "FRCS" (Benjamin Clarke) (1894), reprinted 1986.

Notes

Introduction
1. See e.g. D. J. Olsen, Town Planning in London, (Second edition, 1982), p.31 n.7.

Part One: Estate Development in the 18th Century
Before Development
2. Lysons, Environs of London, (1795), II, p.458; Milne's land use map (1800).
3. Report by James Pennethorne to the Commissioners of Woods and Forests, 1844: V.P.P. vol.1.
4. John Harvey, Early Nurserymen (1974); MDR 1789 6/4.
5. Cf. the incidents of the lease of Hackney terrace registered at MDR 1792 5/627.
6. HAD M. 3589; Robinson II, 381.
7. HAD M. 774; [GLRO] TA/5.
8. JCM 1A/1/7 p.441.
9. [GLRO] H1/ST/E67/1/72; 1/115, 1/81; H1/ST/E/57.
10. JCB D/92; Robinson I. p.206.
11. D/F/NOR/1/1/1-3.

Landownership
12. See note 19.
13. VPP vols 1,2.
14. A. K. Sabin, The silkweavers of Spitalfields and Bethnal Green (1931).
15. Robinson II,381. See also the Report of the Committee on Lammas Lands, St John-at-Hackney (1810) p 11.
16. JCM 1A/1/7 pp 436-448; Robinson II, p 365.

The 18th Century estates
17. [HAD] Z11/3.
18. E.g JCM 1A/1/5, 25 April 1765.
19. Customs and Privileges of the Manors of Stepney and Hackney, 1736.
20. In 1769 and 1780 the Governors of St Thomas's Hospital granted 51 year leases for development in Hackney to Robert Collins and Joseph Spackman respectively: H1/ST/E/1. Thomas Flight's term was identical, and the sub-underlease for Hackney terrace little longer (see below).
21. [HAD] V.29 (1806); JCM 1A/1/6 p. 243.
22. Compare Flight's lease, [GLRO] H1/ST/E67/88/34 and the leases of Gigney's premises in JCB (Jackson's deeds).
23. H1/ST/E/16.
24. On the Grosvenor estate at Westminster the jump from the expectation of 60 years to 99 years seems to have occurred during the 1720's: cf. Westminster archives 1049/3/9/1; 1049/3/9/62. For Camberwell, see H.J. Dyos, Victorian Suburb (1966) pp 43, 89.
25. see note 9.
26. W. K. Jordan, The Charities of London 1480-1660,(1960) p.190.
27. H1/ST/E/103/8; H1/ST/E67/3/30.
28. H1/ST/E/57.
29. [HAD] M.3958 p.84; The Diary of Dudley Ryder, ed. W. Matthews (1939) p.50.
30. H1/ST/E/103/9.
31. [HAD] P/J/CW/62 (1766) and P/J/CW/65(1768). M.3958, "A few lines relating to the Parish

of Hackney", anon., alleges that Shore house fell down c. 1777 or 1778, killing at least one child.
32. H1/ST/E/57.
33. Estate survey 1848 (H1/ST/E/104).
34. HAD P/J/CW/64 (1767). The Diary of Thomas Turner, 1754-1765, ed. Vaisey (1984), p. 345.
35. [HAD] WP4465; note 22 above.
36. JCM 1A/1/7 (17 January 1799).
37. [HAD] V.29.
38. JCM 1A/1/5 (25 April 1765); 1A/1/6A (24 August 1785).
39. Report of St Botolph's Vestry on Sir John Cass's Charity, 1860, Guildhall MSS. 3488.
40. MDR 1788/2/53.
41. [JCB]: lease (4th February 1786); [HAD] mortgage (1787) M.774.
42. Guildhall MSS 19,628.
43. ib; [JCB] Jackson's deeds; MDR 1788/4/501; 1789/4/408; MDR 1789/3/202; 1789/4/331.
44. [GLRO] MJ/SP/1794, January 21.
45. Most of what follows is derivied from the unlisted bundle in JCB marked "Jackson's deeds".
46. Guildhall MSS (see note 42).

Hackney terrace
47. MDR 5/627. The only comparable Hackney development was Buccleuch Terrace (since demolished) at Upper Clapton on Samuel Tyssen's land.
48. Martin Boddy, The Building Societies (1980), p 6.
49. A single copy of the articles of agreement (missing the elevation drawings) survives in JCB, Jackson's deeds.
50. Cf. photographs in the National Monuments Record and the Greater London Record Office photograph library.
51. [HAD] H/LD7/3/2, p. 109. Plots were allocated by lot: Tower Hamlets Archives MS. 2343.
52. MDR 1793/1/88, 1/89.
53. The full 90 are not evidenced on early C19 maps. James Pollard, the freeholder, was by 1798 bankrupt following an unsuccessful embezzlement of public funds: Tower Hamlets Archives MS. 2277.
54. MDR 1797/1/320, 1/321; 1800 1/362; [JCB] lease, Smith to Jackson 1/10/1798.
55. Graves, List of Royal Academy exhibitors, 1769-1904 (1905).
56. Lease, Pickering etc. to Jackson, 1/6/1796 (JCB), memorialised at MDR 1797/2/380. [GLRO] THCS (1800 RB0; [HAD] P/J/M/2 (1797)
57. MDR 1797 3/694;3/235;1798 3/462. No connection has been found between Samuel Ireland of Cannon Street, stonemason, and the contemporary Samuel Ireland, painter and memorialist of Hogarth, or indeed Samuel Ireland & Co., weavers, of Bread street.
58. Country Life, 12 November 1987, p. 192. A similar asymmetry was planned at Sutton place (c.1808): [GLRO] ACC 1876/MP1/221.
59. Glyn Davies, Building Societies and their Branches (1981), p.17.
60. He was the author of the report cited at note 15.

Part Two: Systematic Development
The Influence of the Park
61. JCM 1A/1/43, passim.
62. An excellent account of the Park's early days is Charles Poulsen, Victoria Park (1976).
63. VPP vol 1, and Plans. In The Works of Joseph Paxton, 1803-1865 (1961) G. F. Chadwick suggests that Pennethorne's revisions to his original plan owed much to his coillaboration with Paxton on Prince's Park, Liverpool.
64. The house appears to be that leased to James Ferguson in 1841 for a term from 1837, and

subsequently occupied by Alexander Leighton ([PRO] Crest 2/897), despite the plan attached to the 1843 claim in V.P.P. vol. 1 appearing to have a reversed orientation.

65. VPP vol 4; specifications submitted 2/9/1857.
66. VPP vol 1, 1844. There had been looting of vegetable produce after some gardeners had left. For the replanting order see vol 2, November 1845.
67. Letter to the Commissioners of Woods and Forests, 16 October 1851, VPP vol 3.
68. [PRO] LRRO 64/1; 1851 c.46; [HAD] H/ES/2/85.
69. [HAD] M.3618.

Co-operation between estate owners
70. D/F/NOR/3/7; JCM 1A/1/7 p.441.
71. V.P.P. vol 3, October 1850.
72. JCM 1A/1/10, March 1852.
73. MDR 1851 6/658.
74. [JCM] 1A/1/10, April 1852.
75. [HAD] M.3617; V.33.
76. [JCM] 1A/1/11 p.98; 1A/1/43 5 December 1845.
77. VPP vol 4, April 1855.

The system of building leases
78. [JCB] Orders for leases, 1871; 1893-5.
79. [JCB] building proposals, by Henry Bagge, 15/9/63 and John Wright 12/9/1864.
80. [JCB] The resulting lease was for 90 years from Christmas 1862.
81. E.g. MDR 1862/13/930-4; (1857) H1/ST/E65/125/6; (1856) [HAD] M.833.
82. E.g. MDR 1861/15/507; 1863/17/181.
83. [JCB] Endorsement of 11.9.1865 on Bagge's agreed proposal (note 92).
84. William Norris's was the largest workforce identified: see Appendix 2.
85. See note 92.
86. [HAD] LBH/7/5/4/350; MDR 1862/13/782; D/F/NOR/2/6.
87. MDR/1858/1/279.
88. E.g. MDR 1860/17/1002; 1860/11/512-5; P.O. directories.
89. [JCM] 1A/1/10 (1851); 1A/1/11(1855).
90. [JCM] 1A/1/11 p.485. The making up of Harrowgate road and Meynell road caused contention: 1A/1/12 pp. 125, 330,360.
91. [JCM] 1A/1/12 p.16.
92. [JCM] 1A/1/12 p.156.
93. [JCB]; letter from Sparks, estate surveyor, to Glynes, solicitor, 3 April 1878. The agreement was for a lease of 5 houses in Cassland road east of Valentine road, the site of nos. 41-9, for 80 years from 1866.

Part Three: Gardens into Suburb

Before Systematic Development
94. [JCM] 1A/1/7, 15 .1.1800; Guildhall MSS 19,628.
95. Robinson II, 245; 173.
96. Clarke, p.167; JCB, list of Ridge's underleases.
97. [HAD] 4232/6/2; 4232/7/8.
98. H1/ST/E/16; Robinson II, 367-8.
99. [GLRO] TA/5. If Rocque's map is reliable there was some development along Tryon's place

after the mid-18th century, as the map indicates that Tryon's own development was close to Mare street.

100. H1/ST/E/16; [GLRO] MP1/222A.
101. [JCM] 1A/1/7.
102. MDR 1842 3/835, 3/655, 3/688; 1843/9/558.
103. [JCM] 1A/1/43, 6 July 1846.
104. [HAD] LBH/7/5/3/264; 7/5/25/226.
105. [JCM] 1A/1/43 6 April 1846; MDR 1860/11/571, 1863/9/111.
106. [HAD] M.3561; J. J. Sexby, The Municipal Parks of London (1905).
107. E.g. MDR 1856/7/1027; 1856/13/681; 1860/11/528; 1860/11/326.

The Parr estate

108. [HAD] H/LD7/3, June 1760; M. 1309. A John Wowen was resident in Well street in 1707: [HAD] M.933.
109. D/F/NOR/2/1.
110. Clarke, p. 172.
111. MDR 1834/6/223.
112. [HAD] M. 218-220.
113. See note 109. MDR 1843/5/607; 1843/4/787.
114. MDR 1843/2/725-6.
115. MDR 1843/2/728; 1856/15/218; Robinson II, 297-8.
116. MDR 1843/2/727; [HAD] P.12574-7.
117. MDR 1850/8/866; 1851/14/42.
118. MDR 1851/6/4.
119. MDR 1851/11/688; [HAD] M.2895,2897.
120. MDR 1854/14/889.
121. MDR 1854/15/503; 1855/1/220; 1855/1/997; 1856/11/897; 1857/11/569; [HAD] M.2899.
Turner also appears to have built on the east side of Greenwood's row: MDR 1865/4/238.
122. MDR 1861/6/1014; 1863/11/894.

The Cass Estate

Planning for development

123. [JCM] 1A/1/8, 6.5.1824; 1A/1/43, 28.10.45 and passim.
124. A copy survives in JCB, Jackson's deeds.

Monger's almshouses

125. [GLRO] P79/JNJ/268/2; Robinson, II, 374.
126. [GLRO] P79/JNJ/268/3.
127. [JCM] 1A/1/7, pp. 436, 444, 448.
128. [GLRO] P79/JNJ/267, 7.3.1846.
129. ib. 16.12.1846.
130. ib; MDR 1854/13/88. Compare e.g. MDR 1863/22/1102.
131. [JCM] 1A/1/11, p.244.
132. [GLRO] P79/JNJ/267, May 1848 - March 1851.

"To be let on building leases"

133. [JCM] 1A/1/43, 6.4.1846.
134. ib; MDR 1863/21/577; see also V.P.P, Plans.
135. [HAD] M.3618; [JCM] 1A/1/43 8.1.1847.
136. [HAD] H/LD/3; JCB Old deeds register, vol.1.
137. MDR 1854/3/181.
138. Guildhall Pr.H1/GAS.

Victoria Park road
139. MDR 1852: 3/15, 5/759, 2/766-7; [HAD] WP 2494.
140. MDR 1863/22/1102; 1854/3/29; 1854/7/849; 1855/9/629; 1862/3/853-5.
141. [JCM] 1A/1/11, 8.4.1856.

The northern estate
142. E.g. MDR 1854/3/179-180.
143. MDR 1854/3/179 etc; JCB Old Deeds Register vol.1; MDR 1853/5/457.
144. E.g. [JCM] 1A/1/10, December 1852 and March 1854.
145. ib., April 1852.
146. ib., April 1854.
147. [JCM] 1A/1/11; MDR 1858/1/280-2.

Completing the St Thomas's Estate
148. H1/ST/E/16; [JCM] 1A/1/44, pp 109, 306; [GLRO] TA/5.
149. [HAD] J/BW/E/13/2; V.33; M.3617; V.151.
150. H1/ST/E/114/10.
151. H1/ST/E/40.
152. MDR 1862/13/930-933.
153. H1/ST/E/65/125/6,7.
154. H1/ST/E/65/125/8,11; MDR 1867/21/908; 1875/10/155-6.
155. e.g. H1/ST/E/65/3/10,13.
156. H1/ST/E/65/3/11/1-2.
157. Clarke, p. 175.
158. The road alignments had been surveyed by Currey at the same time as the southern sector: [HAD] J/BW/E/13. See also H1/ST/E/40.

The suburban village: Brookfield road
159. [HAD] H/ES/2/25; Builder's Weekly Reporter, 25 August 1856.
160. MDR 1856/11/974-982.
161. MDR 1857/5/951-7; 1858/8/624; 1862/6/476; 1862/9/258; 1863/1/767.
162. [HAD] LBH/7/5/1, 26 August 1856, 13 September 1856.
163. [HAD] H/LD/7/3. p. 179.

A respectable neighbourhood: Warneford and Fremont streets
164. MDR 1845/10/301; 1851/6/351; 1852/6/355; 1856/4/790.
165. Ratepayers' Journal and Local Management Gazette, 1856-7.
166. ib, 1856, p.45.
167. Land and Building News, 1856, p.431.
168. [HAD] LBH/7/5/2/599; LBH/7/5/4/308.
169. Clarke, p.22; MDR 1855/6/711; 1865/17/272.
170. MDR 1855/6/711.
171. MDR 1845/10/301.

The late 1850's

The Cass estate
172. e.g. [JCB] Old Deeds Register, vol.1.
173. [JCM] 1A/1/11, p.72.
174. ib., p.90.

Frampton Park
175. [JCM] 1A/1/11, p.107. The Frampton house was retained until the 1880's.
176. e.g. MDR 1858/10/561-3, 660; 1859/2/281, 14/241.

Homer Road
177. MDR 1861/12/48-54; 12/465; 1862/5/685.
178. The East End of London, p. 183.
179. MDR 1863/16/183.
180. [JCB] Old Deeds Register, vol.3 (1866).
181. MDR 1860/11/512-5; 17/1002-5.
182. [HAD] LBH/7/5/5/188.
183. [JCB] Old Deeds Register, vol.3; [JCM] 1A/1/12 p. 136.

The Norris estate
184. [JCM] 1A/1/43, 6 July 1846.
185. D/F/NOR/8/2.
186. [GLRO] P79/JNJ/274.
187. [HAD] J/BW/E/13/4; [GLRO] P79/JNJ/301/1.
188. D/F/NOR/2/3.
189. e.g. MDR 1863/17/180-1; 1862/19/232.
190. D/F/NOR/2/6.
191. [HAD] LBH/7/5/7/156, 183.
192. French Protestant Hospital, Charter and Byelaws, (1892), p. xxiii.
193. [HL] H/F/1/6.
194. ib., Wales to Giraud, 15 November 1855.
195. [HL] H/F/1/3; 1/6.
196. [HL] H/F/1/6, Giraud to Grellier, 21 August 1861.
197. Charter and Byelaws, p. xxvi.
198. D/F/NOR/2/6.
199. [HAD] M.1761; Gillian Wagner, Barnardo (1979).
200. [HL] H/E6/7; D/F/NOR/2/6.

Cass: the Final Phase

Exit George Wales
201. Guildhall MSS, 3488.
202. [JCM] 1A/1/11, p.244.
203. ib., p. 361.
204. ib., p. 428.
205. e.g. [JCB] Old Deeds register, vol. 2, 21 November 1863.
206. ib; [JCB], draft agreement.
207. [JCM] 1A/1/11, p. 462.
208. ib., p. 480. [JCB], Orders for Leases, e.g. May 1870.
209. e.g. MDR 1863/18/68-70.
210. [JCB] proposal 12 September 1864.
211. [JCM] 1A/1/11 p. 500; [JCB] Orders for leases.
212. ib.

213. [JCM] 1A/1/12, pp 16-19.
214. [JCB], Orders for leases.
215. [JCM] 1A/1/12, p.111; Orders, as above.
216. See generally, [JCB] Orders for leases.

The Poole estate and Cassland crescent

217. [GLRO] P79/JNI/301/1-4.
218. [JCM] 1A/1/12, September 1865.
219. [GLRO] P79/JNI/291.
220. [JCM] 1A/1/12 p. 230.
221. Thomas Wright took a building lease of Tyler's field which was ended for lack of progress: [JCM] 1A/1/12, January 1870.
222. [JCB], Jackson's deeds.
223. [JCB], bundle of abortive building proposals; [JCM] 1A/1/11, p. 95; /12 p. 326; /13 pp. 375, 412. As the area grew and the Common became popular for recreation it attracted "undesirable characters" until properly paved and lit: George Grocott, Hackney Fifty Years Ago (1915), p. 44-5.
224. [JCB] Directions for leases.
225. [JCM] 1A/1/12 p. 321.
226. LBH/7/5/45/126.
227. Information from Mr S. M. Shaanan, son of Mr Joseph Morris.

Completing the Crown Estate

228. [PRO] LRRO 64/1.
229. VPP vol. 4.
230. Lease 18 June 1860, [PRO] LRRO 64/1; and passim. VPP vol. 3.
231. [PRO] LRRO 1/2200, 2219. Joseph Harris also designed the Royal Hotel for Borton: [HAD] LBH 7/5/280.
232. [PRO] LRRO 1/2269; 64/1. [HAD] LBH/7/5/10/218.
233. [PRO] LRRO 1/2216; LRRO 16/19/37, 14. The other builder concerned was G. Ellson.
234. [PRO] Crest 35/2531.
235. Hackney and Kingsland Gazette, 29 November 1871.
236. The Builder, 28 April 1855, p. 203. [PRO] Crest 35/2531.
237. 3rd February 1872.

Part Four: Living in South Hackney

The sources for this Part have been mainly contemporary directories and census returns.

The residents

238. The suburban homes of London: a residential guide, 1881, p. 197-8; D/F/NOR/2/3.
239. [JCM] 1A/1/11 p.209.
240. [HAD] Z11/3.
241. [HAD] Register of electors, 1834
242. Life and Labour of the People of London, 1902, II.

Estate control

243. [JCM] 1A/1/12 pp. 372,376, 402.
244. See P. G. Hall, The East London Footwear Industry: an Industrial Quarter in Decline, East London Papers [1962] 5, p.3.

Transport
245. [HAD] D/E/257 NEW 11/5; M.3958.
246. 33rd report of the Commissioners of Metropolitan Turnpike Roads, 1859 (GLRO MRC/51); Act of 7 Geo. 4 (1826), c. cxlii.
247. Michael Robbins, The North London Railway, Oakwood, 1974.
248. [JCM] 1A/1/11, p. 499. Letter from Giraud to Grellier, 21 August 1861, [HL] H/F/1/6.
249. [JCM] 1A/1/12/336, 379.

Shopping
250. Information from household bills courtesy of Colin and Sherry Bibby.

Schools and institutions
251. [HAD] H/LD/7/2 p. 109 (June 1791).
252. MDR 1834/6/223.
253. See [GLRO] P79/JNJ/350-1.

Religious and social life
254. Robinson, II, p. 178. [GLRO]P79/JNJ/248/5.
255. Robinson, II, p. 245; H1/ST/E/40.
256. D/F/NOR/8/2.
257. MDR 1865/17/272; Life of Catherine Booth (above).
258. George Grocott, Hackney Fifty Years Ago (1915).
259. [JCM] 1A/1/11 p. 409; MDR 1852/5/759-60; [JCM] 1A/1/43, 12 February 1846.
260. [HAD] WP 2494.
261. [HAD] LBH 7/5/25/226.
262. [JCM] 1A/1/12 p. 310, 326.
263. D/F/NOR/2/3.
264. D/F/NOR/3/1.

Index

Cass family, 17, 61
Cass, Sir John, 18
Cass, Thomas, 61
Cassland crescent, 49, 96, 123 [see also Cassland road]
Cassland Hotel, 114
Cassland house (estate office), 29
Cassland road, 11, 17, 28-9, 35, 46, 49, 68-9, 81, 84, 95-6, 106, 123, 127, 134
Cassland road, nos. 20-54: see Hackney terrace
Catling, George, 95, 99, 124
Cawley road, 123, 127
Cedars, the, Banbury road, 58, 90, 130
chapel of ease, 51-2, 112
Chapman road, 106
charities: see Cass; St Thomas's Hospital; Hackney poor
Chatham place, 53
Chinn, Alfred, 58
Christ Church, Gore road, 112
Christie road, 45, 123 [see also Annis road]
Church crescent, 63 [see also Bellevue cottages, Blenheim cottages]
church of St John of Jerusalem, 55, 61
church school movement, 85, 111
City Corporation, 25
Clarendon Arms, Balcorne street, 42, 57-8, 114
Clark, John, solicitor, 29, 62, 68-9, 81, 91, 124
Clarke, Benjamin, 55, 74
Classic Estates Ltd., 99
Classic mansions, Shore road, 99
Cobeldick, John, 124
Cockerell, Charles, 90, 124
Cole, Edward 124
Collent street, 53
Collins, Robert, 24, 53, 132
Collison, George, 51,
Commissioners of Woods and Forests, 35-7, 40
Common (alias Grove) House, 22, 29, 60-61, 99, 111
Common, Well street: see Well street common
congregational chapel, Cambridge Heath, 113
Connor street, 17
Cook, William, 68, 124
Cornwall road, 123
covenants in leases, 28, 107, 116 [see also building leases]
Cresset street, 53

Cubitt, Thomas, 52
Currey, Henry, 41, 70, 72, 74, 86, 90, 111, 115, 124, 136
Currie, James Neil, 55
Currie, Malcolm, 55
Cuzner, J. H., 72

Dabell, Joseph, 79, 124
Dagmar road, terrace: see Danesdale road
Dagmar arms, 114
Danesdale road, 94, 122-3, 129
Darnley road, 25, 74, 123-4, 126
Davis, William, 57
Day, George, 69, 84, 91, 124
de Kewer, 112
de la Pierre, Paul, 55, 110
Deerfoot cottages, 101
Denmark place, Well street, 52, 72
Denmark villas, Shore road, 72, 123
Derby road, 93, 123, 126-7
Devonshire roads, 25, 74
Dolphin pub, Mare street, 83, 113
Dornbusch, George, 101
Dupree, William, 55, 114
Dyer, W.B., 95, 102, 125, 130

Eagle, William, 17, 53
Eagles, the, Well street 26
Earl Derby pub, 114
Eastman, Hugh, 44, 47, 67, 84, 86, 100, 125
Edwards, Robert, 49, 95, 125
Eleanor road, 125
Elephant and Castle pub, 83
Elizabeth Fry Refuge, 112
Ellson, G., 138
Elsdale street, 47, 53, 68-9
employment, 104
Empress of India pub, 54, 115
enclosure of common, 69
Ennor, Thomas, 100, 125
Evangelical Association for the Propagation of the Gospel, 51, 111

Falcon and Firkin: see Queen's Hotel
Feast, William, 79, 125
Fellowes, William, 30, 32, 33, 51
Ferguson, James, 133
Fern villas, Victoria park road, 49, 67
field boundaries, 42
Fletcher's gardens, 29, 59
Flight, Thomas, 26, 43, 47, 132
Flying Horse pub, Mare street, 113
Fowell, James, 90
Fox, Samuel, 52
Framingham, Christopher, 70
Frampton arms, 114
Frampton, Dr Algernon, 22, 82, 105
Frampton estate, 41, 45-6, 73, 82, 106, 112, 122, 124-5, 129
Fremont street, 11, 40, 42 [see also Warneford street]
French Academy, Well street, 110
French Hospital, 87
Fricker, Henry, 92

Gardner, Thomas, 76, 125
Gascoyne road, 49, 65, 97, 106, 125, 130
Gatfield, Gedaliah, 26, 48
Gibson, Jesse, 27, 81
Gigney, William, 28, 30, 51, 59
Gillespy, Thomas, 69, 73, 81, 91, 125
Giraud, Mr, 88
Glaskin road, 82, 86, 130
Glaskin, T. P., 45-7, 72, 82-3, 88, 93, 107, 122, 125, 127
Gloucester road, 127, 130
Goldsmiths' and Jewellers' Almshouses, 58
Goldsmiths and Jewellers Annuity Institution, 57
Goodman, James and Josiah, 97, 126-7
Gore road, 102, 113, 122-3
Gotha street: see Warneford street
Graham road, 126-7
Green Dragon pub, Well street, 113
Greenwollers, Charles, 27, 59
Greenwood, Thomas, 102
Greenwood's row, 53, 73, 111, 130 [see also Kingshold road]
Grellier, William, 61
Griffiths, W. P., 57
Groombridge road, 22, 90, 127-8

Grosvenor estate, 24, 116
Grove cottage, 29, 63, 68, 99 [see also Limes, the]
Grove house school, 97, 111 [see also Common house]
Grove road, 18, 36, 38, 53
Grove street, 17-18, 27, 35, 53, 55, 105, 124, 129 [see also Lauriston road]

Hackney Bay, 35, 51, 59
Hackney brook, 17, 76
hackney carriages, 108
Hackney Literary and Scientific Society, 115
Hackney poor, charities for the, 17 [see also Monger, Poole, South, White, Vyner]
Hackney terrace, 20, 30-34, 59-62, 70, 96-7, 108, 132
Hackney Theological Seminary, 56 [see also Evangelical Association]
Hackney vestry, 37, 125, 130
Hackney Wick, 54
Hacon, H.D., 52, 70, 72
Hakewill, E. C., 61, 85, 112
Hall, Sir Benjamin, 77
Hambro' synagogue, 22
Hamilton, Thomas, 27, 45
Hampden (Baptist) chapel, 55, 112
Handley road, 39, 71, 86, 129
Harman, James, 74, 83, 89-90, 123, 125-127, 130
Harman, James, junior, 124
Harman street, 126
Harris, Joseph, 100, 123, 138
Harrowgate road, 44-5, 93-4, 106, 122, 128, 134
Haynes, J., 79, 126
Heart place, Cassland road, 17
Heath, Thomas, 57
Hedger, George, 39, 41, 54, 76
Hedger's grove, 76, 106, 125-6, 128
Herring, Frederick, 89
Hertford Union canal, 38
Hickling, Jonathan, 80
Hickling, Zillah, 22, 77
Holcroft road, 46, 56, 127, 130
Holt, J. and W. S., 83
Homer, J. J., 83, 113, 126
Homer Road, 83, 106, 125-6
Homer terrace, 83
Homer, W. R., 83

Ridge, John, 21, 51
road-making, 49
Robinson, Thomas, 55
Rockmead road, 125, 127
ropeworks, Cassland, 65, 105, 115, 128
Roumieu, R. L., 89
Rowe and Timpson, 77-8
Royal Hotel, 115, 123, 138
Royal Standard pub, 67, 100, 115, 123,
Russell, Charles, 96
Ruthven street, 95, 125
Rutland road, 93, 123, 126-7
Ryder, Dudley, 26
Ryder family, 104

Sacker, Joseph, 53
Saunders and Field, 129
Scholtes, John, 87, 90, 95, 129
Schools, 110
Sell, Thomas, 29
servants, 105
sewerage, 103
Shafton road, 95, 125, 130
Sharman, Henry, 107
Sharon Gardens, 99
Shearman, William, 129
Sheffield family, 44
Shillitoe, John, 30, 32
shoemaking industry, 107
Shoobert, John, 17
Shopping, 109
Shordych, Elena and Sir John de, 18, 25
Shore house, 18, 35-6, 48
Shore place, 25
Shore road, 18, 25, 40-41, 47, 70-72, 106-7,
    123, 125, 128, 130
Shoreditch place: see Shore house
Shoreditch place estate, 23
Shuttleworth's hotel, Well street, 52
Silk Mill row, Cassland road, 54, 76, 106
silk mills, Hackney Wick, 19, 54
Sir George Duckett's canal, 36, 38
"Sir John Cass" pub, 66, 114, 126
Sir John Cass's charity, 11, 20 [see also
    Cass estate]
Skinner, F. and A., 129
Skipworth road, 39
Smith, Alfred and Job, 130

Smith, Thomas, 29
Snooke, William, 75
Society for Promoting Christian Knowledge,
    85
Sotheby, Captain, 21, 36
soup kitchen, 112
South, Richard, 17 [see also Hackney poor,
    charities for]
Southborough road, 49-51, 86-7, 89, 106, 123,
    127, 129-30
Spackman, Joseph, 132
Spackman's buildings, 27, 132
Spanish and Portuguese Synagogue, 22
Speldhurst road, 71, 86-7, 127, 129-30
Spurstowe road, 125
St Agnes terrace, 41, 100, 125
St Augustine's church, 101, 112
St Botolph's, Aldgate, parish of, 91
St John of Jerusalem, church, 41, 112
St John of Jerusalem, Knights of, 16
St John's terrace, Lauriston road, 56, 58
St Joseph's Hospice, 46
St Pancras, Marylebone and Paddington
    Freehold Land Society, 76-7
St Thomas's hospital estate, 18, 20, 23-5, 36,
    41, 52, 70, 82, 107,
St Thomas's place, 24, 27, 52, 130
St Thomas's (Ainsworth) road, 40, 70-1,
    73, 93, 122, 128-30
St Thomas's (Skipworth) road, 102
St Thomas's square, 24
St Thomas's square chapel, 55, 113
stabling, 31, 76, 94, 100, 108
Stanley road, 74, 129-130
station, Homerton, 108
station, Victoria Park, 82, 108
street names, 14
Stuart House, Cassland road, 113
Suburban Villa and Village Association, 75
Suffolk road, 87
Sureties, Joseph, 28
Sutton place, 133
Swiss Cottage pub, 54, 113